W9-BSU-367

The
Motivation
Process

FROM THE
LIBRARY OF:
Jerry Parzych

WINTHROP MANAGEMENT SERIES

William H. Brickner, *Series Editor*

BRICKNER AND COPE

The Planning Process

CAMPBELL

Understanding Information Systems: Foundations for Control

ENDS AND PAGE

Organizational Team Building

ROCKEY

Communicating in Organizations

SANFORD AND ADELMAN

Management Decisions: A Behavioral Approach

SCHAEFER

The Motivation Process

The Motivation Process

Susan Davidson Schaefer

Winthrop Publishers, Inc.
Cambridge, Massachusetts

Library of Congress Cataloging in Publication Data

Schaefer, Susan Davidson.
   The motivation process.

   (Winthrop management series)
   1. Employee motivation. I. Title.
   HF5549.5.M63S3   77-76801
   ISBN 0-87626-583-2

Cover illustration by Ruth Williams.

Photographs by Scott Brickner.

© *1977 by Winthrop Publishers, Inc.*
17 Dunster Street, Cambridge, Massachusetts 02138

All rights reserved. No part of this book may be reproduced in any form or by any means without permission in writing from the publisher. Printed in the United States of America.

10 9 8 7 6 5 4 3 2 1

contents

three

Incentives and Rewards   61

four

Punishments and Stress   91

five

six

seven

eight

editor's preface

Energy crisis! Political crisis! Personal crisis! Economic crisis! . . . . I believe they all have a common element: *mismanagement*. It may be mismanagement of resources, mismanagement of everyday activities, mismanagement of organizations large and small, or mismanagement of societies in general; however, it is becoming increasingly clear that many people do not manage well.

If we define management as planning and using resources such as time, money, energy, etc. to attain stated objectives (goals), then the ability to manage well can have a significant impact on almost every life experience. We conceived the Winthrop Management Series with the idea that the basic skills and principles necessary for successful managing are not complicated; almost anyone can learn them. With a basic understanding of these skills and principles, people can become more effective managers at all levels: in large organizations, in small groups, or in their personal lives.

WHO NEEDS 'EM? (MORE BOOKS ON MANAGEMENT, THAT IS)

We have directed the books in this series primarily toward those people who would like to do a better job of managing, yet who have neither the time nor the inclination to enroll in a full program of management courses at the university level. The authors have written the books to be used individually, or as a set, in industrial training programs, community colleges, university extension classes, or as focused readings in undergraduate or graduate management courses. In addition, the authors hope that the books will provide useful self-study material for those people who learn on their own by reading daily.

Organizations in all areas of society are growing larger and more complex. As a result, individuals with a wide variety of backgrounds and vocations are recognizing the need to learn the principles of good management. Hopefully they can benefit from the Winthrop Management Series. Experienced professional managers also may see these volumes as an aid in successfully carrying out one of the most important managerial duties, that of helping subordinates to manage *their* jobs more effectively.

WHAT THIS SERIES IS ABOUT

The books in the series are concerned with those skills which experienced managers find most critical for developing a successful managerial career. The results of a nationwide questionnaire to 266 top and middle managers in business, government, and nonprofit organizations are shown in the following table. The managers ranked these skills and per-

Skills		Personal Attributes	
Leadership and Motivation	18.7%*	Ability to Work with Others	22.5%*
Information Systems	11.6%	Drive, Energy	21.7%
Communication	11.2%	Adaptability to Change	11.9%
Understanding Human Behavior	10.8%	Intellectual Capacity	11.9%
Finance	10.4%	Ability to Communicate	10.4%
Awareness of Environment	7.1%	Integrity	8.4%
Planning	6.4%		

*Shows relative weight assigned from 100% total.

sonal attributes as most important for long-term managerial success in the future.[1] Accordingly, the authors have examined many of these skills and attributes in these six series volumes:

1. *The Planning Process* by Brickner and Cope.
2. *Understanding Information Systems: Foundations for Control* by Campbell.
3. *Organizational Team Building* by Ends and Page.
4. *Communicating in Organizations* by Rockey.
5. *Management Decisions: A Behavioral Approach* by Sanford and Adelman.
6. *The Motivation Process* by Schaefer.

Communication, decision making, and the ability to motivate oneself and others are process skills important to all managers. The books on planning, organization building, and control through information systems include the most important functions that managers perform. Although the six books do not discuss all of the many topics involved in management, we feel that they cover the most important ones.

MAJOR SERIES THEMES

One of the main themes of the Winthrop Management Series is the concept of *systems* or *processes*. Management is not a series of unrelated activities. Like the universe, management is an interlocking rational system governed by "laws." The fact that many of these laws are "undiscovered" should not detract from the principle that management is an ongoing process. This process involves inputs of resources and infor-

[1] Brickner, W.H. *The Managers of Today Look at Those of Tomorrow*. Presented at the National Meeting of the Academy of Management, Seattle, Wash., August, 1974.

mation, the shape and form of which are changed, resulting in some outcome. Information about the outcome (feedback) is then compared with the desired outcome (objective). If the comparison is unsatisfactory, the inputs or the processor are changed. The following diagram illustrates this concept:

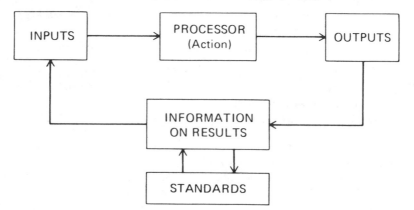

Each of the topics covered in this series is actually a smaller system, or process, that is a part of the overall system of management.

Another key concept in organizing the material for these books is *Pareto's Law*. This "law" states that a relatively small percentage of the inputs creates a large percentage of the outcomes. (For example, 20 percent of a firm's customers may be responsible for 80 percent of its sales volume.) With regard to the series, each author has organized each book around a few specific ideas which he or she believes to be the major keys for successfully mastering each basic process discussed.

The application of principles and theories to real-world situations is an extremely difficult problem for many people. To help bridge the gap between theory and practice, each volume contains a *Panel Discussion* of several successful management practitioners. They are individuals with varied backgrounds who in their careers have successfully used whatever management process they were talking about. The panelists addressed themselves to the problems and opportunities which could result from applying the theories discussed by the author in the preceding chapter of the book. The resulting dialogues are rich in insights and guides that can aid both novice and experienced managers.

ACKNOWLEDGMENTS

Many people have been involved in the creation of the Winthrop Management Series. However, one person above all made it possible. My personal gratitude goes to Michael Meehan, our editor at Winthrop Publishers, Inc. Mike provided early encouragement when the series was but a faint idea. Subsequently as this idea became more tangible, he was willing to "put his money where his mouth is" and support the publishing of the six volumes.

The help which these books will provide to managers is the result of the unstinting efforts of a creative team of authors and panelists, each of whom contributed to the series the knowledge of a lifetime of managerial experience. They all took time out from very busy professional lives to share this knowledge with others. My thanks to each of them.

William H. Brickner
Series Editor
Los Altos, California

author's preface

This is a book about motivation. It is intended to approach the subject in a way that is realistic and usable since ideas about managing don't have much meaning unless they help to make better managers. Thus, the emphasis is on developing ideas which a manager can learn and, consequently, put right to work in his or her own supervisory situation.

Managing is not a "secret" process. A person who is new to the role can become a good manager; the experienced manager can always improve his or her performance. Learning to understand employee motivation is an important aspect of learning to manage. So the question, "How do I motivate employees?" will be addressed from several different directions to develop the ways in which knowledge of motivation can be put to use.

In keeping with the "real-world" focus of this and other volumes in the Winthrop Management Series, a panel discussion by practicing managers forms an integral part of the book. This discussion is not a review or critique of the text. It is a presentation by successful managers of their own beliefs and behavior in motivating employees. Their contribution is immeasurable. Editing more than four hours of conversation covering a wide range of topics was a challenge. They questioned, even argued with each other, developing ideas in a wholly spontaneous fashion, with frequent bursts of laughter greeting the perceptive or humorous remark. In acknowledging assistance, I must first thank them.

I appreciate, as well, the help of other authors in the series, particularly that of Bill Brickner and Don Cope, in helping to recruit the discussants. Dr. Harold J. Leavitt, Walter Kenneth Kirkpatrick Professor of Organizational Behavior of the Stanford Graduate School of Business, offered valuable help and encouragement, and provided me with the format of Chapter Two as well. A number of people helped with typing, but special thanks are due to Louise Nelson, who struggled with most of the transcript, and to Sandra Anderson, who arranged for the transcription and typed various drafts herself. My husband Jerry prodded occasionally, sympathized often, and managed to detect those invisible-to-the-author errors.

Finally, I must acknowledge the valuable editorial assistance of my husband's mother, the late Bernice Schaefer, a teacher of language arts. The energy she put into early drafts of this book was expended in the face of an increasingly severe illness. It is to her memory that this work is dedicated.

Susan Davidson Schaefer

The
Motivation
Process

one

Motivational Models

OBJECTIVES

When you have completed this chapter, you should be able to:

1. Name the principal models of motivation, which are used in understanding on-the-job behavior, and describe their important features.
2. State the features these models have in common.
3. Select the model that most closely resembles your personal understanding of the motivation process.

GLOSSARY

Behavior   An activity of a person (or other organism) which can be perceived by others.

Goal   An object toward which a person strives.

Model   An object or situation similar to an object or situation being studied, which can provide information or understanding of the subject of study.

Need   A lack or deficit within a person.

Theory   A set of generalizations which can be used to describe observed events or predict future events.

APPROACHES TO MOTIVATION

Supervisors often ask, "How can I motivate employees?" Although this is a common question and an important one, it is not easy to answer. This book will explore answers on several levels; however, the concept presented in this first chapter may be a surprising one. For in one sense, a supervisor *cannot* motivate employees. To understand this fact we must understand what motivation is all about.

Motivation, simply stated, is why people do what they do. Understanding motivation, then, is an important key to managing people. A manager who knows why he or she and other people behave as they do will be more able to solve problems. The individual will also be able to predict what will happen when a decision is made or when something changes in the organization.

People have always wondered why others act as they do. Philosophers have speculated about this for centuries, and from their reasoning have come such concepts as *free will* and *predestination* to describe this important *why*. More recently, psychologists and even biologists have studied the physical and mental processes involved. Too, systems theorists have tried to identify the motivating factors common to all systems, whether they are simple such as a single cell or complex like a human being or organization.

Over the years, two basic approaches to motivation have evolved. Both are based on the very general statement, *people do what they do because something pushes them.* The difference between the two is essentially the origin of the push. One position holds that the push comes from outside the person. The other says it comes from inside. How is this different? Imagine someone making you the following offer: Here is a large room kept at a comfortable temperature. It contains a bed and a complete bathroom. There is a place in the wall next to the bed from which nourishing food will come at frequent intervals. You may live here rent free for as long as you wish; however, you may bring nothing with you and nothing more will be provided. You will not be disturbed by anyone.

Perhaps now the difference becomes clear. The two motivation theories attempt to predict how long you would stay. The *outside* theory says that there are no forces pushing you to act. In the absence of rewards for doing anything else or punishments for not doing anything at all, you would stay forever. As long as your bodily needs were met you would be content to lie in bed. The *inside* theory says that this lifestyle would get boring very quickly. We all might welcome a few days' rest, but inside each of us are many needs, hopes, and plans that just cannot be fulfilled by lying in bed. Douglas McGregor calls these two approaches Theory X and Theory Y.

This extreme example may clarify things, but it may also introduce another question: Is what's true for me true for others as well? We are often tempted to say, "Well, I would get bored, but I know someone who wouldn't, or most people wouldn't, or some kinds or groups of people wouldn't." Another problem that may arise is that of confusing *why people do what they do* with *why people do what others want them to do*. We say, "My son is lazy, because he won't do his school homework (what I want him to do)." But in fact he may be very industrious in what he *does*—practicing the electric guitar or rebuilding a car engine. We will see how such ideas may influence our view of "correct" motivation theory and where the evidence to support the theories really is.

NEEDS

In general we may think of the motivation process as one in which a force causes action. The force is based on *needs* or *wants*. We would consider statements such as, "I need a new pair of shoes," or "I need friends," or "I want to be president" to be expressions of this force toward action. We then can say that people have needs which cause them to behave in order to reach some goal (or fulfill some need). We would diagram those elements like this:

However, it is important to remember that we cannot see inside people's heads. We can only observe what they do. So the needs and goals which motivate behavior (what the person does) may often be hidden from us. We see only external behavior and must infer or assume what the needs and goals involved might be. The process really looks like this:

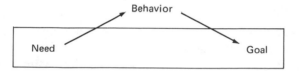

Everything other than the behavior is in a black box so that the workings are not available for us to see.

Some psychologists divide needs into two basic categories—*primary* and *secondary*. This division is generally based on whether the need is *physical* or whether it is *learned*. Thus drives such as hunger or thirst would be primary; they are physical needs and we are born with them. Social needs (for example, the desire to be with other people or to be liked by them) would be secondary. The dividing line between primary and secondary needs is sometimes difficult to perceive, however, because there is not always agreement on which needs are learned.

The diagram of the motivation process described earlier suggested that needs are the first component. So it is necessary to examine what those needs are. We will consider some motivation models which relate the different needs.

Maslow's Model

Probably the most well known model of the relationships between needs is that developed by Abraham Maslow. In his scheme, needs are related in a *need hierarchy* which is usually represented like this:

Maslow's position is that people have needs or wants inside them which cause them to act (so this is a Y-type theory). People act to fulfill needs which are important to them at a particular time. For example, the basic needs (at the bottom of the hierarchy) are physiological (physical); these are the primary needs we just discussed. When these are not met, nothing else matters much. A scuba diver who is running out of oxygen, or a person lost in the desert without water, will single-mindedly pursue those immediate needs. Other physiological needs include food and shelter. However, suppose that a person's physiological needs are satisfied. Maslow believes that *satisfied needs no longer motivate behavior*. Thus the physiological needs, when they are satisfied, do not cause people to act, and the next level of needs takes over. In Maslow's scheme, the next level includes the *safety* needs which are related to providing security. For example, after a hungry person has eaten, the individual becomes concerned with the basic physical needs on a regular basis and the sense of security that follows.

Suppose then that a person has a place to live and a

job—thus providing for the safety needs. What will motivate the person to act beyond this? Maslow states that at
this point the *social needs* become important. These needs
involve being around people and being accepted or liked
by them. When social needs are satisfied, the *esteem needs*
are next in line. These needs involve a person's feelings
of worth or importance. We must be careful here, however.
If a younger brother says to you, "You're the best basketball player in the world," that is really a statement which
fills a social need. He is telling you he likes or admires you,
but he is really not able to judge performance. If the coach
says, "You're a very good basketball player," this is information about your real worth. Esteem needs are fulfilled by
recognition, a sense of accomplishment, or a feeling of a job
well done.

Up to now all of the needs have been active or striving
needs. That is, you are outwardly active, or do things that
can be seen in order to achieve them. The remaining needs
are those of *self-actualization* or those which Maslow refers
to as *being-becoming* needs. These needs are related to becoming more of what you are—more of a person, more
mature. Maslow, however, felt that not many people reach
a level at which self-actualization is the primary motivator.

Remember that at any point in time behavior is motivated
by several different needs simultaneously. The hierarchy
simply represents the progression through which we move
as we mature. For example, in a developing country a person who has just emerged from poverty may behave in ways
which indicate that the individual is fulfilling needs like this:

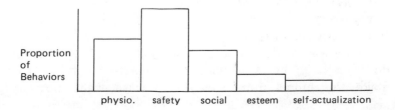

So a great deal of time is spent fulfilling safety needs. The person still must devote some activities to physical needs, but social needs are beginning to be important at the same time.

Now consider an American, a middle manager in a manufacturing business located in a large city. What might this person's need hierarchy look like?

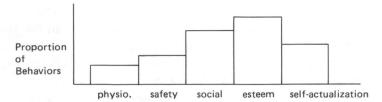

This individual has physical and safety needs mostly taken care of and therefore does not have to devote very much time to them. Most of the needs are for esteem—knowing that what he is doing is valuable and that his contributions are worthwhile. In fact Maslow has suggested that there are some people for whom the desire to make important achievements is so great that it must be fulfilled before social needs. This might be "the man in the gray flannel suit" who became infamous in the 1950s.

This discussion may give you a clue to the nature of the need hierarchy—it is definitely a *model*. The person is a black box, and we infer or reason out what goes on inside from what we see externally. In the motivation model what we see is *behavior*, and we must deduce what causes the behavior. It is no different from the reasoning process we use when we see someone running down the street. We speculate whether the person is hurrying to meet a friend or escaping from a police officer.

Maslow's model is a general picture of why people do what they do. A manager or supervisor may want to make this model more specific to learn what motivates people with respect to work behavior. The models which follow will deal specifically with motivation at work.

Herzberg's Model

Frederick Herzberg's model represents one of the most popular work models. Herzberg began to notice differences in people's responses when asked what they liked about their jobs. Sometimes they answered that things like high pay, good supervisors, or fringe benefits were important. At other times they seemed concerned with recognition, opportunities for advancement, or the status of the job. After further investigation Herzberg found that the various responses were the result of slightly different questions. When workers stressed the importance of pay or company benefits, usually they had been asked some variation of the question, "What things about your job make you unhappy if they are unsatisfactory or completely missing?" Those who were more interested in the value of the job had been asked questions like, "What makes you want to work harder or better?" Herzberg concluded that job factors could be divided into two groups. One set (he called them *dissatisfiers*) includes job aspects which make workers unhappy, generally those things labeled as "working conditions." However, even if these conditions were adequate, they still did not serve as incentives for action. The real *motivators* were items such as recognition, job importance, and the opportunity for advancement.

If we compare Herzberg's findings with Maslow's hierarchy, some interesting similarities emerge. The dissatisfiers—sometimes called hygiene factors—resemble either the safety needs (job security, good pay) or the social needs (a good supervisor, pleasant working companions). The motivators, on the other hand, resemble the esteem needs. Therefore Herzberg's research seems to show that safety and social needs are relevant to people on the job, in that if these needs are not met people become dissatisfied and seek improvement (or other jobs!). Yet the factors that stimulated behavior desired by the company or supervisor, such as working harder or better, seem related to esteem needs. So it seems likely that many people in organizations devote many actions to fulfilling esteem needs. It will be important to remember this later on.

McClelland's Model

Another model of work-related motivation is that of David McClelland. He studied the basic needs and concerns people frequently express and divided them into three groups: the need for *achievement*, the need for *affiliation*, and the need for *power*. Everyone has each of these needs to some degree. A person with a high need for achievement is of particular interest to the supervisor or manager. Such a person desires to set moderate goals and strives to achieve these goals. The individual enjoys taking some risks and seeing the results of actions taken. These needs and desires are interesting because they coincide with characteristics of successful business executives. People who are achievement oriented often choose and are successful in managerial careers.

Vroom's Model

Another useful model, that of Victor Vroom, does not consider specific needs but rather the choices between alternative actions. Vroom believes that people perceive what they do as important in achieving "outcomes." A person's motivation level is based on *expectancy* (the probability the

person sees of accomplishing something and of being rewarded somehow for the accomplishment) and *valence*
(how strongly the individual values the accomplishment
and the reward). Thus a person might be highly motivated
to go to night school if the individual strongly desires a promotion, expects to do well in school, and sees further education as directly related to the promotion.

AN OVERVIEW OF THE MODELS

We have examined several models of human motivation.
Based on research these models have in common the assumption that motivation comes from *inside*. That is why
one answer to "How do I motivate employees?" is "You
can't." However, Chapter Two will show how internal
motivation may be modified by *outside* influences. The
models also share the assumption that so-called *higher-order
needs*, needs beyond the physical level, exist. These models
do not deal with how people fulfill higher-level needs, but
that is not really too important now anyway. Most people
already have those higher-level needs, whether they were
born with them or learned them as infants. Too, the models
make similar guesses about what the important human needs
are. The two which seem to appear again and again and with
which we will be concerned are (1) the desire to be with
other people and (2) the desire to accomplish worthwhile
things.

Chapter One has been concerned with *theories* and
models. It will serve as a base for the material in later chapters. However, the most important thing about a theory is
its USEFULNESS. Indeed a theory should help us *describe*
or *predict* something. The law of gravity, for example, is a
theory which describes the behavior of objects under given

conditions and predicts what will happen to them. It allows us to say, "If I hold this baseball out the window and let go of it, it will fall to the street." Similarly, the motivation theories should help us describe what people do and predict what they will do. This is a very powerful skill for any manager to have.

Theories and models are tested by research. In hundreds of studies and experiments, both in the "real world" of offices and factories and in controlled laboratory settings, speculations or hypotheses about human motivation have been and are being tested. The successful ones become part of the body of theory and in turn (along with the mistakes, which make scientists more curious!) generate new hypotheses.

These, then, are not "pie in the sky" theories about what might be in the future or about the world as we would like to have it. They are called *descriptive* theories, because they describe and explain things as they actually exist. Therefore it is important for the manager to be familiar with these theories, since they can be useful in a number of ways. First, they help focus attention on real, basic human needs as they might be exhibited on the job. Accordingly, they give the manager something to look for. Second, they may help the manager clarify his or her own feelings and opinions about motivation, and to rethink past assumptions which might not have been tested. Finally, and we will explore this in more detail later, these theories serve as guides to managerial action. If people have needs, then knowledge of this will help the manager to better understand their behavior. Too, the manager who can recognize that people's needs differ can "tailor" his interactions with subordinates more suitably. Therefore, managers have much to gain from a thorough understanding of the motivational models. We will rely on this understanding throughout the rest of the book.

SUMMARY

Motivation is why people do what they do. Even though people over the ages have speculated (Theory X) that motivation comes from outside the person, the biological and psychological evidence favors the position (Theory Y) that people do what they do because of needs and wants inside themselves. These are generally roughly divided into primary and secondary needs. Various people have proposed models to indicate motivations more specifically; most of these models include a small number of classes of needs, which all of us have to some degree.

SKILL DEVELOPERS

1. Examine what you *do* (your *behavior*) for two separate hours during one day—one, the first hour you get up, another, an hour during your working day. Use one of the models to analyze what *needs* each of your actions fulfills.
2. How good a descriptive theorist are you? Here is a list of needs a person might have (you will recognize them as patterned after Maslow's hierarchy):

    security   friendship
    accomplishment   emotional maturity
    self-fulfillment

    Rank them in order of importance to you (1 = most important, 5 = least important). Then copy the list on a sheet of paper and give it to someone you know well (spouse, parent, child, or best friend). Ask that person

to do the same thing. While he or she is working, you try
to predict the person's rankings. Check. How well did you
do as a predictor? And how similar were your own personal rankings and those of your friend?

3. Ring Toss: Play a game with yourself. Set up a bottle and
get a jar ring or any other kind of ring to throw at the
neck of it. You may choose how far away you wish to
stand. Observe yourself and see whether you stay in the
same place, or whether you move back as the task becomes easier.

REFERENCES

MASLOW, ABRAHAM, "A Theory of Human Motivation." *Psychological Review* 50 (1943):370-96.

PANEL DISCUSSION

Each book in the Winthrop Management Series contains a discussion of its important concepts by real-world managers. The panelists for this book, all residents of the San Francisco Bay Area, prepared for the discussion by reading a draft of the text and reviewing a set of general questions about the importance of motivation in their own managerial work.

The principal discussants were Jerry Zones, Lynne Zittle, Bob van Horn, and Phil Quigley. Jerry is General Manager of Perky Pies, a subsidiary of Del Monte Corporation, and has successfully developed several businesses. Lynne is Coordinator of Patient Services for Kaiser Permanente Medical Center in Santa Clara and is experienced in supervision related to health care. A former line manager, Bob van Horn is director of corporate development for Saga Corporation, a Menlo Park–based food service corporation which was actively involved in the research of Abraham Maslow. Phil Quigley, whose past experience has been in such diverse areas as the Marine Corps and sales management, is a consultant and part-time instructor in industrial relations.

The editor of this series, Bill Brickner, helped in taping the discussion and also was a valuable participant. "Sue" refers to the author.

In this section, the panelists discuss their views of the meaning of motivation and consider Theory X and Theory Y.

Sue: We're going to be talking today about motivation, and I thought maybe I could get you to spend a little while talking about what motivation means or how you use the word. I think I'll start with you, Jerry.

Jerry: O.K. I'd like you to clarify motivation. What are we talking about? What level and what type of people are we talking about? Are we talking about young people out of college, or are we talking about entrepreneurs that are

Sue Schaefer

Jerry Zones

Phil Quigley

Bob van Horn

Lynne Zittle

Bill Brickner

part of large corporations, or are we talking about corporate people who are coming up through the chairs of the corporation?

Sue: Well, hopefully, we could be talking about any of them.

Jerry: Well, I think you have different motivations depending. Take a guy like Bob who's been with Saga for 19 years. He's gone through the chairs. A guy like myself, or my counterparts, that sold my business—for lack of a better term—I'll call myself an entrepreneur. How do you motivate people like us, in a large corporation which is an alien environment because of the corporate structure? So, if you can clarify what you're talking about—if the book is primarily directed to the younger, middle management who are going to come up in the corporate world, I think we should direct ourselves to that.

Bill: Yes, I think so, because I think that that's where the bulk of the activity will be—the people that go back to junior colleges. You know, the bulk of them will be in larger organizations, not necessarily corporate, but governmental, too; but they'll be in larger organizations. That's where most of our managers are.

Jerry: I would say, I guess, stature and remuneration. Hopefully, eventually that they can get to the point where they are self-achievers and that's the ultimate in motivation. But I think until one gets into that classification of being a self-achiever, I think that they've got to be financially comfortable. The culture's changing so rapidly. The young managers from my personal experience have somewhat of an idealistic attitude. In fact, I just went through an experience with a very bright young man; we had a parting of the ways after 14 months. A very capable young man, and basically we had an ideological difference; and we're still very good friends. In fact, I'm trying to get him a job; it's very interesting that you bring up this subject because we had our parting of the ways last week; and it was quite traumatic, but I was forced to sever the relationship before we got to be enemies. I don't know if I've answered your question.

Sue: You've given us a lot of food for thought.

Phil: I was going to say that to me it's kind of important to distinguish between movement and motivation. Because, when you talk about motivation, to me it means activating somebody's inner generator—getting somebody to do something because they want to do it, not because you want them to do it necessarily. For managers that creates kind of an interesting problem because most managers that I have encountered, and even as a manager myself, typically what I've wanted from my people has been movement rather than real motivation; and I think you have to determine whether you want to manage truly motivated people, because that's a very difficult process—to manage truly motivated people. In most cases what we really want is movement. We want people to do what we want them to do. What we tell them to do. We want predetermined behavior. So, I guess, the general working definition for motivation that I use is activating that inner generator—helping to create a climate that will encourage people to motivate themselves, because you really can't motivate anybody else. I can no more motivate Jerry than he can motivate me. He can create a climate for me that will encourage me to seek the goals and objectives that I identify with, but motivation as a word is a difficult one because it implies that somebody can control. As Bob said, to set up predetermined behavior patterns is pretty difficult.

Lynne: I agree with you. I don't think that we can motivate anyone else and we can't make them be motivated. We can model for them and perhaps it will be contagious.

Bob: But you can find their hot buttons and then set a climate so that you push that button and get this behavior.

Lynne: Depending on whether your style appeals to that individual or not.

Bob: That's if you're compatible. As Jerry found out that he wasn't. Attitudes, needs, behavior—those are all three just kind of one—a oneness of words. And when you're talking about trying to motivate somebody, it's finding out which one of those tools you use to get what you want out of that person. Make him want, or he or she want, it.

Jerry: Anyway, my style of managing is that I tell my people what I want accomplished—the goal—and then I let them use their own style; even if that may be completely alien or distasteful to me, but you can't expect people to emulate yourself or do it your style as long as they're doing the job. That's what counts. And it's kind of tough. And then you have to let them make mistakes, and you back them up—but you let them know you don't expect them to make the same mistake twice because you don't tolerate stupidity.

Bob: That's called management by objective. You set the objective and he gets there his way.

Jerry: Right. If I feel that I've been successful in discussing the strategy, then I would voice my opinion negatively or positively, but I don't expect them to be influenced by my opinion. Even if I know that they're going in the wrong direction, if it's not too severe of a catastrophe economically, I let them do it because it's all part of training, and training costs money so you well can afford it.

Lynne: How do you hold yourself back from jumping in when you see them going in the wrong direction, or what you feel is the wrong direction?

Jerry: You bite your tongue and you just watch like big daddy. You know, you tell the kids, "Keep your hands off the stove, it's going to burn." They're still going to put their hands on it the first time and you feel for 'em and that's about it. And it's a matter of measuring, and what mood you're in that day, also. It's a matter of self-discipline, basically. Because if you don't have that discipline, you're not going to be a good manager and you might as well go out and do it yourself. And you don't get anywhere doing it always yourself. You can only get so big and that's it. So, basically, it's a human resource problem. You've got to be a psychologist, you've really got to get involved and try to get on a personalized basis, not socially but where they come from and what their thinking is.

Sue: I'm curious about something that I hear. Do you feel that your own view or the manager's own view of what people are, some sort of philosophy, has something to do with how you manage? I almost heard, when Jerry talked, some feeling about "what is another person?" emerging. Somehow the style you would pick would depend on your view of "mankind." I don't like to use such global terms but . . .

Phil: I think what you're really talking about now, Sue, is some of the things that Doug McGregor said in terms of Theory Y. The view of man as a thinking, learning, growing animal pretty much describes Theory Y, which is a sanitized way of expressing that man is a growable, learnable animal, and really does want to work, and does want to succeed, and does have real needs for fulfillment other than strictly monetary. Theory X, of course, implies that the guy is lazy and needs to be prodded and shoved, either cajoled or kicked or wheedled, and when you, as a manager, look at your people, I think you have to have a fundamental feeling for whether these people are really learning, growing kinds of individuals that if I create the right environment will jointly commit to the goals that we identify or do I have to kick them all the time? And I think any manager basically has to come to that conclusion. Do I have to push and pull my people or carrot and stick motivate them, or can I create a free-wheeling climate which will enable them to develop and motivate themselves?

Bob: As a manager, you've got to know when to do one or when to do the other. Theory Y is, you know, 90 percent of the time, the best way to go. But at times when you're talking about survival or economic interests of your organization, then you as the manager have to make that trade-off and say, "This one will be Theory X because I say so."

Phil: Theory Y and Theory X don't necessarily mean that you kind of zig-zag between the two. If you're a Theory Y manager you realize that occasionally you'll have to take very firm decisions and you won't be able to consult or participate. But if your attitude is "most cases I'll participate and consult with my people because they've got good ideas," then essentially you're following that same orientation. As Bob says, sometimes you don't have time. Management by participation is very difficult (and very time consuming) and very frustrating sometimes, because they don't always come up with the ideas you want them to. And they bring up things that really are irrelevant and they bring up old stuff from their own experience within the organization.

Phil: I have a client company that I consult for in Palo Alto and they have what they consider to be a very forward-looking personnel function. They're always coming up with great new ideas and they said, "Well, why don't we come up with a new policy that will enable people to take a leave of absence, come back with a guaranteed job after six-nine months?" And I said, "That's a great idea, but can you really do it? What if the guy is a marginal performer? Can you reinstate a marginal performer? What if you have a cutback and you have to lay people off? How will you accommodate this?" And their problem was that they were letting their people come up with all these great ideas. Well that's where, in a sense, you need some guidance and Theory Y can sometimes run amuck. I think an unbridled Theory Y kind of philosophy can lead you down the straits.

Lynne: You can also pretend Theory Y and just turn out to be a phony.

Phil: It's like the old suggestion box.

Jerry: If you pretend Theory Y, you will find you'll build up a tremendous amount of resentment at your staff meetings, and frustration, and then you get an attitude—what are we going through this crap for; let's knock it off.

Lynne: Time to cut the garbage out. He'll do what he wants to anyway.

Jerry: Right. So then you don't get participation. So it's a very tight wire to straddle.

Sue: Well, Lynne, it would seem to me that you have a double level of this view of people; because not only does a person who is managing in your situation have employees to manage, but you're also trying to give the employee some sort of view of the client and how you want them to feel about or act toward people that way.

Lynne: I think the majority of our people are there because they're caring individuals. They may not necessarily be dedicated to the way they handle the paper, but they're there because they want to help people. And some of them will go off and do it in their own direction, which is not necessarily the way the organization is going. But I think in management, in motivating people, that a lot of it comes from the manager himself—how he feels about himself. Does he like himself and trust himself and therefore can he like and trust other people? If you hate yourself, that comes across; and you can't be free and open, you can't trust other people.

Sue: One's own motivations, then, would come into . . .

Jerry: Oh yeah, one's own motivation—especially one's own inner security and I shouldn't say self-respect, but self-confidence is the word.

Lynne: How about self-esteem?

Jerry: You've got to build that confidence. Naturally no one is going to tell you, especially if he's got 15 years' tenure with a company, that he doesn't have confidence; so, they've got on a facade.

Lynne: But how did you go about breaking through the facade?

Jerry: Well, in very simple terms, I have a way with very simple street language which seems to break a barrier, put on a very common level, that I'm not the big-time executive— I mean that's my personality. I'm fairly fluent with the four-letter words, and I've been using this as a tool for many years and it works—for me, anyway. It's just speaking it the way it is. That there's really no big deal about production, and that basically you do know it. It's the unknown that scares people.

Phil: People really relate to the basics. I can see how Jerry's particular style would really break through because so often people build up this mental image about something they don't know about, and all the buzz words and the zip words, the generalizations that they can't penetrate and all the inside jargon . . .

Jerry: Right. Here's a young man who starts off with the company, and he starts off in the sales training program and he gets on the street and sells and he's moved around about 12 times and he's gone up the ladder. Now he's made vice president of a company. He's always looked up to the executive as the president. I mean, it's kind of scary. So you break this level down like—we're human beings; we put our pants on one leg at a time, and all we have on you is experience, maybe some breaks—you're just as bright as I am. You basically build their confidence.

Bob: But at different levels of the person's career—this is for people coming out of college, going into corporations. Different motivational techniques work at different times with different people. You've always got to understand where they're coming from. And here we're talking about the 20–24-year-old person who's joining the corporation. You have one level of needs that generally they want satisfied first, and it's good pay and a good job and a career ladder. And once they get on that career ladder and things are going well and they're beyond whatever their minimum level of existence is for their style of life, then you've got to use something else to motivate them and then you get into prestige, self-esteem, job challenge, job growth; and you're filling out the whole person as a person, not just the person as a subsistence level. And so, throughout all these things when you talk about motivation there's no commonality because everybody comes from a different place and wants to get at a different place.

Bill: Sue, I was called away for a minute. Did you cover or have you talked about the problems of people who are just entering the workforce—not from a college, not even, perhaps, from high school, but maybe broke off after a couple of years in high school or something like that? There are a lot of new people in the work force these days that aren't necessarily college graduates or even high school graduates.

Sue: Let me open that a little further. One of the areas I told you we would talk about is difficult situations to manage. I think that this would definitely fall into that category, whether you're talking about what we referred to some years ago as the "hard-core" unemployed, or whether you're talking about a person with less formal education than we tend to think of as being the norm these days, or someone perhaps regardless of educational level who's in a first job and simply isn't tuned in to the world of work. I think Bob started to say something about wages being something that people start out thinking are important.

Bob: Yeah, that's the first thing. That's the most important thing because wages are just a tool. That's the good thing about money. It motivates people for many different reasons. Jerry might buy a boat, and I'll buy a bigger house, and Lynne will buy more cosmetics or something; but money gets to all of us. And so, in the beginning money is very good motivationally because people can buy their car or whatever their bag is. They can use money to do it. But after they get all those things, then more money doesn't motivate them that much more. There's no correlation at all.

Lynne: I think there's a hard-core individual that Sue was speaking of. You bring them in, they're hired, they're told how much money they're going to make, and then I think we owe it to them to tell them exactly what we expect of them, how they're going to be measured.

Phil: You know, there was an interesting phenomenon about five years ago. The auto companies took a lot of those people from the ghetto in Detroit, brought them out to the plant, put them to work, because they needed to fulfill their quotas for affirmative action reasons. They gave them pretty good starting salaries, and they were working 18-20 hours a week overtime at time and a half and sometimes double time; and they found that even though those basic needs were being taken care of, there were still problems because what they had really wanted to do was to hire people who wanted to start at the bottom and stay there. So they didn't really develop any kind of a meaningful career ladder for these people because they were supposed to be, in a sense, at the lowest-paid menial jobs. And so whenever you do deal with anybody on a first-job basis or hard-core unemployed, it seems to me in the orientation you've got to

give people a viable picture of where they can go up within
the organization, and hopefully . . .

Bob: Even if it's nowhere, even if it's nowhere. Right?

Phil: That's right.

Bob: I was going to talk about that when I talked about
motivation today—something about our society, particularly for the male, says that if you're well motivated you
compete and you win; and a lot of people, males, play
football or something like that and they get used to winning, playing on a team and winning; and the natural suc-
cession for them is to go into business, play on a team, and
win. And you can measure winning. You know when you
have and when you have not.

Phil: In fact, that's one of the things that kids are taught in
team sports at a very early age—win at football now and
you'll win as branch manager for IBM in 10 years.

Bob: You keep score in order to determine who *does* win,
too.

Jerry: Look what a success Lombardi was. He's got a big
business, like a Dale Carnegie thing. And he's done fantastic
things with large corporations. The name of the game is
win. They go out on seminars, a lot of the ex-football
players, and it's a big business that they've got going.

Bill: Well, that is true in business—that you tend to look
at things more as a team effort than just an individual player,
where in academia—most academics, I think, look at it as an
individual effort and people who are oriented toward being
individual contributors tend to go into academia. I—at least
in the years I've taught and I've done some teaching in two
or three places—have not seen much in terms of team spirit
and when I was department chairman, trying to get people

to think in terms of doing something as a team—as a department—extremely difficult.

Bob: How do you tell whether Stanford won as an insti-
tution?

Jerry: It takes years and years.

Phil: There's no feedback.

Jerry: But we don't always have the weekly scores in business either, you know; it all depends on the strategy. You
have a long-range plan and a short-range plan. And a short-
range plan is fairly easy to measure. The long-range plan you
can't measure until you hit your goal. During the developing period, it's pretty painful. You get tired of losing money
even if you knew before you went into it you were going to
lose for five years. And about the third year you begin to
wonder, "Hey, am I on the right track?" Then what do you
do? Do you keep pouring more money into it? Because you
can start having doubts. When you develop a new market or
a new product, and products just don't take off. The fatality
is unbelievable. You talk about the 95–90–85 percent range
of fatalities of new products. And the cost—the waste.
The amount of money that's expended on losses is unbelievable.

Bob: But what it does to your team.

Jerry: The spirit is unreal.

Lynne: So you're in the ideal situation. You're on a winning
team and the profits are high and you're working 14 hours a
day, 7 days a week. What happens to you as a human being?

Bob: You thrive on it.

Lynne: Do you?

Jerry: Oh, there's nothing like saying, "Boys, we did it," especially if it was a long shot.

Bob: That also changes as people move in cycles of their life.

Lynne: What about the successful man who has a bleeding ulcer and instead of going on vacation, he's in the hospital; he has a nervous breakdown?

Jerry: Then he has second thoughts, but if he had to do it all over again he would do it all over again.

Bob: And it might have happened to him no matter what kind of job he had. Ulcers are more prevalent in low jobs than in high jobs.

Jerry: That's right. The job doesn't give you the ulcer. It's the personality that gives you the ulcer.

Bob: It's the type A behavior.

Phil: We induce our own tensions, I think.

Lynne: But is it worth it?

Jerry: That's in each individual's own decision. They get smarter and they know how to moderate it and how to handle it.

Lynne: Mellow out a bit.

Phil: Learn to live with it.

Sue: You sound kind of doubtful.

Lynne: Well, no. I'm just thinking in my own mind about the women's movement and so on, and all of a sudden women are finding out what it's like to be in a competitive race.

Bob: Sure, the suicide rate is going up and the death rate's going up and everything like that.

Phil: The divorce rate.

Lynne: I, too, feel more pressure than I did five years ago; that's for darn sure; and I can't help but have some empathy for men to think they have been living in this all of these years and women have been settling back and saying, "What's the matter with him; he's grumpy again!"

Jerry: It's so easy to be critical.

Lynne: But women are now having the reality or experiencing the reality of . . .

Bob: See, now they have a choice where we, as men, pretty much wanted to live the programmed life and didn't have a choice. Women are in a wonderful place. They can say yes or no.

Lynne: Oh. Some women really can't. If they are like men, competitive, they have climbed out on a limb far enough that they can't choose.

Bob: They are more committed then, too.

Bill: What motivated you to get into management, to move into a management position? What motivates you to stay out there?

Lynne: I've done this much, I want to do more. I like to win, too. I like to be on top.

Jerry: Has it affected your femininity?

Lynne: No, I don't think so.

Jerry: Have you been told, by others, by friends?

Lynne: No. I've been told that I use my femininity in business.

Jerry: Well that's what everybody uses—whatever they've got. So that's par. I don't find that offensive.

Phil: No way.

Jerry: Because men use whatever they've got so this is part of the game.

Lynne: I'm more aggressive than I used to be, Jerry.

Jerry: Yeah, well, you should be.

Lynne: I'm not as dependent as I used to be. I've had a tradeoff. I can stand on my own two feet.

Phil: This sounds like a pretty good tradeoff though. You really gained in the process.

Jerry: Yeah, oh yeah. You're not relying on anybody; you can handle it. You could take on the world by yourself.

Lynne: Yes, that's right.

Jerry: Which is very healthy as a human being; we all should be that way.

Sue: Well, I don't know about that either. There is an interesting article in the Journal a few weeks ago about two-career marriages. And one of the things they pointed out that really struck home to me was about needing support and needing to say, "Guess what happened to me at the office," and the problem of two people coming home from opposite directions and one of them says, "Boy, I had a terrible day at the office," and the other one says, "Wait until you hear what happened to me!"

Phil: "Don't tell me about it, let me tell you about mine!"

Sue: This happens at our house a lot; and I think that we all have this wishful thinking that it would be nice to be able to stand on our own two feet, but most people have support, and traditionally I think what we've done in our society is that we've adapted, for management people, the theory that hourly workers ought to leave their needs at home. We've adapted that to say, okay, management people, supervisors, can take their competitive need or their achievement needs to work; but they ought to leave their social needs and their affiliation needs at home. So you go to work and compete and then come home and affiliate. If nobody at home is sitting there waiting to affiliate, it's a different situation than what we've traditionally pictured—for men, I think, particularly. Bob, I'm wondering about something related to this. You've talked a lot about winning and hands on and being out there where it's at. I think I heard you say you shifted into a staff job. Do you find that different?

Bob: Very different.

Sue: Did you prefer that old day-to-day . . .

Bob: Well, I was seeking a lifestyle change, which doesn't mean it doesn't come without frustrations. The rewards are less and the amount of responsibility is less. There's not much you can measure, you know, so it's very frustrating.

Jerry: So you made your tradeoffs.

Bob: I made my tradeoffs. I had to adapt my way of thinking and my method of management to it.

Jerry: But one has to face the reality that you don't get everything you want out of life.

Bob: But now I give a good report or something like that and that's got to be my kicks. It's not a big sale or it's not a great month or anything like that. It's just got to come in a different way. Nine months from now because of that beautiful report that I wrote, I see some behavioral changes in the company. I sit back and say, "A little bit of that's mine." It's difficult to get into that frame of mind.

Sue: Do you think you're going to find that, ultimately, you're going to want to go back or can't you predict at this point?

Bob: I don't want to say, "I'd never go back" unless I can, and I'm not ready to give that answer yet.

Bill: I guess this point of knowing yourself or what turns you on and what gives you a payoff as an individual whether you're on the line or a manager or you're top executive, it's just very critical. The staff manager has to recognize that he has to work through other people, and if he can't do that, if his kicks come from being able to take action directly, he tends to be unhappy because he doesn't get that reward and therefore he's not motivated. It doesn't get reinforced. The same is true in long-range planning. If you have to have immediate rewards and you're in a job where the rewards don't come until three or four years down the pike, and that's true in teaching too, very frequently, then you probably are not going to be motivated to do a good job because the nature of the job does not meet your own motivational need. I think that's sometimes when people get in trouble shifting from line to staff.

Phil: That happened to me on my first job out of the service, selling typewriters for IBM and at that time guys were going into computers. "Well, Phil, you can make a lot more in computers," and I said, "But the time from the moment you first call on a customer until the time that he actually closes the order might be two years"; and I said, "I'm only selling a typewriter that might be a $600 to $800 item (IBM's typewriters are pretty healthy), but I get reinforcement every day." Typically if I've done my job, I've sold several typewriters and I've made a major contract or I've made a good presentation. I can walk out and say, "Hey, I did it by myself." It was a solid contribution and accomplishment. The guy that sells a computer makes a hell of a lot more money than I do. On the other hand, he may not sell as many computers and he doesn't get that kind of ego reinforcement that I got and that was so important to me. I'd be happy selling ice cream bars as long as I'm doing it every day.

Lynne: Because you get that constant feedback.

Phil: That's what turns me on. It's a sense of accomplishment.

Bill: How do you get that in your present activities?

Phil: It's a lot more difficult, because I don't sell a consulting program every day. So I get it from doing a very good job for the clients that I have, and I find that I like consulting because I like to recommend and develop the system and come up with the strategy and implement it— then get the hell out. I don't want to stick around and see how it goes. Hopefully it goes okay or I won't get any more business, but I like the diversity of the things that I do; the different kinds of industries. That, to me, the variety, the challenge, the different situation is what turns me on.

Jerry: I think the thing you get out of all our conversation is that a person's really got to know themselves, what turns them on. Are they happy in what they're doing? That goes down even to the lower management. Even though they have goals of getting up, they have to enjoy. This is the key.

Lynne: I've found in my job in the last few months I have finally become aware that I've had a lot of frustrations because I'm used to being a doer and being involved with a lot of people and I'm somewhat removed now. I've had to stop and think about, what is my job today? Is it coordinating these people to get work done through two or three levels rather than just one or two levels, and I found myself thinking, "Gosh, I'm really not doing anything any more."

Bob: "How will I know when I'm doing my job well?"

Jerry: But one of these days you'll look and you're gonna see all these departments are running smooth and say, "Hey, I've done my job."

Lynne: Well, I can see some team effort coming out of this.

Bob: Turnover goes down.

Jerry: Because you're doing your job.

Lynne: Well, I have to stop and talk to myself on occasion, because here I am sitting, or I'm just out wandering around with people, and I'm not doing a specific task.

Bob: The strongest discipline necessary is when you're bored. You tend to do something if you're a doer. That's the worst motive to do something—because you're bored.

Sue: I found this interesting. I shifted from being out there in the real world to being a teacher. Where again you're never done. The student goes off and you never find out that he rules the world because of something you told him. Even though I've had mostly staff jobs out there, nevertheless, you still had a heck of a lot more feedback than you do doing what I'm doing now.

Phil: The nature of most organizations is that you start as an operator in a doing kind of capacity, then make your move into a key responsibility contributor kind of guy. Then you move into management. People are channeled into that management role. You know, it was always assured. You start off as an account representative. Then you get to be a district representative. Ultimately you get into management. I said, "Gee, what happens if you don't want to get into management?" "Oh! You don't want to manage other people?"

Bob: We made a bad hire!

Phil: Really, I like to sell and make money, play golf, not management; but I think a lot of times people move into that role who haven't really ascertained what their motivations are. They grab that rail and ride along with it; and a lot of people, I suspect, are misused in the corporate hierarchy because they may be functioning as managers but they would really rather be a salesman or an engineer or a research scientist or an administrator; but we get socialized into that hole. I know I did it. I felt guilty about it because I was a crappy manager. I enjoyed selling much more. So much more exciting to me and fulfilling. Then I became a creative incompetent, by spending a lot of time selling with guys that weren't selling very well. So I reinforced their inadequacies and helped my own along. That wasn't a good idea.

Sue: Well, I think that was one of the topics that I really hoped we would hit on—an understanding of what people's own personal motivations were—and I suspect that what we've got is, in a way, what I had thought we might find. We were trying to pull together people who were very results-oriented, which is why we were looking for you folks. We certainly appear to have done some of it. We've talked a lot about doing and achieving and this sort of thing. I think that again is something that is oriented toward the kind of people who are going to be reading this.

Bill: Now this is the reason that Lynne made the comment about really having to get to know your people, and several other people here did too. One of the principal things that you get out of knowing your people is you do find out what turns them on. If you're insightful about asking the right kind of questions over a period of time you begin to see what kind of people they are and sometimes get them to know themselves, too.

Phil: People very often don't really analyze what it is about themselves that turns them on. I know I've always kind of gone along, kind of decided this seems to be the best path without really challenging it or asking why.

Bill: The outsider frequently does that better, because he sees you from a different perspective. You see yourself from the inside looking out, and the guy outside looking in sees you a lot differently and has insights that you'll never see, and that's true of all of us, whether again we're on the line or in the chairman's chair.

two

Influence

OBJECTIVES

When you have completed this chapter, you should be able to:

1. Name the principal methods of influence.
2. Understand the characteristic strengths and weaknesses of each method.
3. Describe a situation from your own experience in which you could use each influence method.

GLOSSARY

Human Relations An approach to management which focuses on morale as the key to productivity and thus concentrates on fulfilling social needs on the job.

Human Resources An approach to management which focuses on participation in decision making (for better information and ideas, as well as fulfillment of esteem needs) as the key to productivity.

UNDERSTANDING INFLUENCE

In Chapter One we noted that sometimes we can say, "He's not motivated," or, "Theory X must be true," because the person we are referring to is not doing what *we* want. Sometimes we confuse *why people do what they do* with *why people do what we want them to do*. The first is motivation.

NOTE: The arrangement of this chapter and influence categories follow those of Leavitt, *Managerial Psychology*, 3rd ed.

The second is *influence*—the process by which a person's behavior is affected or modified. Let us look at two simple examples of influence, both using children. Suppose we see a baby reaching out, from curiosity, to touch a hot stove. We quickly give the child a toy. We are diverting the curiosity, this desire to explore, from something dangerous to an object which will be just as interesting to the child, but safer. We have changed the child's behavior. The child, however, is still responding to the desire to explore. Or suppose that a child does not want to go to bed. He says, "I want to stay up to watch T.V. with you." When we say, "You can help me plant the garden tomorrow if you go to bed now," (perhaps such bargaining is not a good child-rearing practice), we are recognizing the child's need (in this case, to be with adults and feel grown up) and proposing a substitute behavior. When we say, "I'll take you to the zoo tomorrow if you eat your lunch," we are eliciting a behavior *we* want in return for doing something the child wants.

Influence, then, is obviously related to motivation. In each case the child being influenced has needs or wants. The influence either provides possible behaviors to fulfill these needs or offers to fulfill them in exchange for some desired behavior. We might want to consider some further implications of Theory X and Theory Y. If influencers (perhaps leaders or managers) believe that Theory X is true, they probably think that it is up to the influencer to provide motivation, to create the cause for behavior. We often think of this concept as "carrots" and "sticks." The manager says, "Do this and I'll give you a carrot" (a paycheck or a promotion) or, "Do that or I'll hit you with a stick" (give a reprimand or terminate). Theory Y, on the other hand, provides a different view of the role of the influencer. Assuming that each person already has needs and wants, the influencer acts as a director or channeler, showing the person being influenced how to fulfill needs by exhibiting behavior desired by the influencer (achieving the goals of a work group or a business firm). The philosophy identified in Chapter One thus affects in important ways how you try to influence others.

MODELS OF INFLUENCE

We can place *influence* in four basic categories: influence by authority, influence by coercion, influence by manipulation, and influence through collaboration. Each method has its own characteristics, strengths, and weaknesses.

Authority

Influence by authority is perhaps the simplest to describe. It is the way one person gets another to behave in some way because that person has the *right* to do so. The state police can require you to put chains on your car in a snowstorm because there is such a state law to be enforced. The police have a legal right to influence you. Some rights are traditional in a culture—parents usually have the right to tell their children what to do even after they are too big to be spanked! Some rights to influence come from relationships which are similar to legal rights—that of the Marine drill instructor or the boss of a business. When a person joins an organization, whether it is the Army or a business firm, the individual agrees (like an informal contract) that some people in the organization have the right to give him orders as a condition of the membership.

It is easy for those with authority to forget that the person being influenced has something to say about it. If a person believes that the influencer does not have the authority to give orders, the person may just ignore the orders. Too, there may be situations in which a person has the authority to tell us what to do in some ways ("Have this sales report in by 5:00 P.M."), but not others ("and while you're at it, shine my shoes."). So the *right to give orders* must be accompanied by the *acceptance of that right* by the people to be influenced. Otherwise, they will ignore the influence, resist it, or perhaps even leave the situation.

Authority has its limitations as a method of influence. You must have it before you can exercise it. (Of course, you may get it by age, expertise, or delegation, as well as by law, contract, or tradition.) Moreover, the people you are dealing with must agree that you have got it, or you will be ignored or undermined. On the other hand, authority is fairly easy to use; it is understandable and direct and it is uniformly applied. A supervisor may have to say to a friend, "I sure hate to do it, but if you are late for work once more I will have to notify payroll to dock you."

Remember that people vary in their responses to authority. People who have been influenced by authority over a long period of time may grow to rely on it. People who are frequently criticized or disciplined may feel that authority is safer, because they are always told what to do. Obviously a person who is frequently disciplined may see individual initiative as very risky.

Coercion

So far we have been talking about the right to command. However, there are times when someone gives an order without authority. One of the most familiar is, "Stick 'em up." *Influence by coercion* uses some means to threaten the limitation of another person's options if orders are not followed. Usually the means is a powerful tool (a gun, a bomb, superior

physical strength) or sheer numbers (there are more of us
than of you); but it also may be anonymity. The strength of
a blackmailer or kidnapper is that this person has something
you want, but you cannot identify or locate the villain.

The user of coercion holds sway by saying, "Do this or
I'll . . . ." Often the threatened action is outside or just on the
border of what is legal or permitted in the society. However,
that does not mean that only "bad guys" use coercive measures. The Montgomery bus boycott and the housewives'
meat boycott were attempts by legitimate groups to use their
numbers to influence others over whom they had no other
authority. Similarly, during the growth of the American labor
movement activities such as strikes, which are now widely
used as bargaining tools, were by law illegal. Thus a strike
by a union to gain society's recognition was technically
illegal, whatever it was morally. Often an "out group" may
use coercive measures to penetrate the power structure of
an organization to further its aims legitimately from within
the structure.

The use of coercion to influence others has several drawbacks. It requires powerful tools or large numbers, and it is
often resented and resisted. Also it is likely that when the
situation changes or the means is lost, the influence is lost
as well. And coercion is sometimes illegal. On the other
hand, coercion is very fast, and there are situations, particularly for individuals or groups who have been defined out of
other areas of influence, where no other method is available.

Manipulation

Influence by manipulation is the most commonly used
method of influence. Manipulation is getting people to do
what you want them to by making them think it is what they

want or by taking advantage of your relationship with some person. We manipulate in many situations even when we have authority or coercion available, too. For example, it would be offensive to always give direct orders ("Bring me a box of paper clips!") or to always threaten our children ("Come here or I'll spank you!"). Instead we say, "Since you're going to the supply cabinet . . . ," and, "Mommy would be happy if you'd come here." Manipulation is not usually uniform; we alter our approach based on what we know about the person to be influenced. Unlike coercion, manipulation is a gradual process.

Manipulation occurs frequently both in business and in personal relationships. We use our knowledge of other people and our relationships with them to get them to do what we want. Often the people are not aware of being manipulated. We know enough about them to make them feel that they themselves want what we want. Whenever we talk about "making somebody *feel* like" he decided something for himself, we are talking about manipulation.

Manipulation is used so often that sometimes we do not even notice it. However, the major drawback is that when people *do* notice it, they resent it and are wary the next time around. When a new "friend" only wants to sell you something, you may feel "taken." Yet manipulation has the great advantage of being available to everyone without special training, techniques, or qualifications. That is why it is so widely used.

Collaboration

The last method of influence is quite different from the others. In the previous examples, most of the work or effort was done by the influencer who does something to the person being influenced knowing specifically what it is he wants done. In *collaboration*, the fourth category of influence, most of the emphasis and the effort is on the part of the person who is being affected. In collaboration the person being influenced must recognize the need for change, consider the alternatives, decide what needs to be done, and act accordingly. The influencer is primarily an adviser, pointing out the need for change or helping to create alternatives. But the actual responsibility lies with the person being changed. Organizations like Alcoholics Anonymous, which stress their role as helpers not "pushers," are typical users of the collaborative approach. For some problems such as alcohol addiction, collaborative influence is the only method that works. If you have ever tried to lecture or nag another person to quit smoking, you are aware of this.

Collaboration, then, is a method which tries to *really* do what manipulation pretends to do. This approach encourages the person being influenced to take charge; to plan and carry out real, important decisions. In any situation, business or family, it is a time-consuming procedure. And it may be frightening, because neither the influencer nor the person being influenced really knows how things will turn out.

Collaboration has one very real advantage over the other methods of influence. When people are *involved* in a change and are making their own decisions, better, more lasting, and less resisted change usually results. On the other hand, the person to be influenced must recognize the problem. (What happens if the individual says, "I don't see any problem?") A *specific* solution cannot be imposed. Of course these conditions might be drawbacks. The individual being influenced will do what *he or she* thinks best and may consider and reject the solution the influencer actually had in mind. Whether these are in fact drawbacks depends a great deal on the situation. The crucial element seems to be trust.

Consider an example of each method of influence in action and observe how they differ. Suppose you have just been hired as a shop foreman. You notice that several workers you supervise consistently come in late. Shortly your boss tells you that he has noticed it too. It is your job to influence the offenders to change their behavior. Using authority you may say simply, "From now on, you guys are going to be here on time!" This statement implies, "I have the right to tell you when to come to work." Coercive tactics might be less effective in this instance, but you could say, "The next guy to come in late will be assigned the worst jobs for a week!" A manipulative tactic might be, "C'mon, you guys, I'll treat you right if you'll help me keep out of trouble with my boss on this," or, "When you come in late the guys in the shipping room have to stay late." A collaborative approach would be to simply state, "We have a problem. A lot of people are coming to work late." The solution might end up to be a petition for flexible work hours or a rule set by the group, depending on the actual causes of the problem and the ideas for a solution.

Certainly it would be helpful to pinpoint one of the methods as "best," or suggest one that should be used all the time. But it just is not possible. Coercion is fastest, authority (when you have it) is simplest, manipulation is used most often, and collaboration produces the most lasting change. And each has its drawbacks. There is no firm "rule" about which one to use. We must analyze the setting and the consequences. Again we are concerned with gaining the ability to *predict the result* of an action, in this case to predict someone's response to influence. The successful manager, knowing the conditions and relying on experience as to the reactions to the influence methods, will pick the method which will produce the most desirable set of consequences.

As a manager, you may have a choice of the methods available to you. You may find, for example, that people accustomed to the traditional methods of management pre-

fer to influence and be influenced by authority. Manipulation
may be used in situations where several people are vying for
power or a promotion. Younger people and often professionals
like scientists or engineers may respond best to collaborative methods. However, there must be enough time to use
them effectively. It is important to make conscious decisions
about the methods to be used in a particular influence situation, just as it is important to consider carefully any managerial action. Too many managers develop the habit of
using the same influence method, regardless of person, setting or problem. As a result they are not as effective as they
could be. Frequently an influence method is chosen for
the wrong reasons. For example, many traditional "how-to-
manage" books assumed that men and women were very
different in their motivations, that women were too sensi-
tive to authority and should be influenced by manipulation.
While it is true that people differ in their responses to influence, there is very little support for the idea that the
difference is based on sex.

Before leaving the influence methods, we should note
one similarity which will become important later. The collaborative influence process is related to the concept of
"participation" in organizational decision making. Raymond Miles has called the utilization of employees' untapped ideas and abilities the "Human Resources Concept."
This position assumes that most employees have skills and
knowledge which the organization does not fully use. Using
this untapped ability leads to a more productive or profitable organization, the more collaborative solution in this
case being of higher quality because the people who actually
work with the problem help to solve it. In the process the
esteem need is fulfilled simultaneously.

Miles differentiates this position from one he calls the
"Human Relations" approach. In this approach, participation is viewed as serving to fulfill the social needs of em-

ployees. They are permitted to participate in limited ways, not because their contributions are viewed as valuable, but because participation will make them "feel" like they are a part of the organization. It is essentially a manipulative influence process. The cynicism with which employees greet suggestion boxes or meetings in which the ideas developed are never used indicates that the manipulation is recognized and resented.

SUMMARY

We can classify the many ways we use to influence people into four basic categories—authority, coercion, manipulation, and collaboration. Each has advantages and disadvantages and each is related directly or indirectly to the motivational processes of the person to be influenced. One of the motivational challenges faced by a manager is the necessity to select a method of influence which is most appropriate to the setting, the problem, and the person to be influenced. Another answer to "How do I motivate employees?" is "Managers channel motivation through the use of influence."

SKILL DEVELOPERS

1. Think of something you might want other members of your class to do—vote in the next election, lend you their class notes, or whatever you suggest. Suggest how you would apply each of the four influence processes to attempt to influence the class members to do this. Which

do you think would work best? Remember, the one that will work best depends on what behavior you want to influence!

2. Think of three people—one a personal relation (friend, relative), one someone "above" you in your work organization, and one someone "below" you. Consider a situation in which you wanted that person to do something. How did you exert influence? How did it work? *NOW* think of how that person influences you.

REFERENCES

MILES, RAYMOND. "Human Relations or Human Resources?" *Harvard Business Review*, July–August, 1965.

PANEL DISCUSSION

In this section, the panelists discuss their relationships with employees and how they influence subordinates. They consider that the appropriate method of influence may vary according to the situation or the individual being influenced.

Bob: As people go up in a corporation the rewards that are available just because you are a big company are fewer and fewer, and it is very frustrating to try to keep somebody turned on, the team turned on; give them all the money they need, any more they wouldn't change their lifestyle, they'd just have tax problems. You've given them all the good press; you've given them a big title; now what's left, you know, to give them, to reward them?

Jerry: Now the only thing I find at that stage that's worked for me is I give them the Theory Y, participation in decision making.

Bob: Just dump responsibility on them. Just fill 'em up.

Jerry: What I have found works very, very well—you have these—the department head meetings and you throw things at them and you get everybody's idea and you plan a strategy and there's no doubt about it that the captain of the ship usually tries to direct the strategy. But I usually am the last one to talk, and I let everybody speak. And then, you'd be surprised, sometimes you come up with some good ideas, but even if you don't you get them involved. Then, they know what the goal is. They come up, try to help to achieve this goal. But this is not easy to do.

Phil: I think you have to be careful when you do that because sometimes people will perceive participation as another form of manipulation.

Bob: If you always wait until you're the last one, they're going to say, "Well, we'll spend a little air time here and Jerry'll tell us."

Jerry: You can't force your method on others. That's the biggest fallacy and the biggest problem we have with managers because then they want to get the "X" routine. They're just shooting out orders. They're not growing. They're not building anything.

Phil: Yeah. It's very difficult for a man who's very results-oriented because you know, he had a certain objective and he has human resources to reach it. It's very difficult for a guy—sometimes to restrain himself because he can see the easy way. The individual doesn't learn as a result of that and I think all managers, I know as a manager myself, I always want to reap the glory and manage the organization and drive the engine. I liked being a captain in the service because, man, I had responsibility. I could tell people what to do. I didn't have to participate or commit. It was so easy. Sometimes a manager has to hold himself back. I know I do all the time.

Jerry: Very important.

Lynne: Jerry, you talked about being "big daddy." What does that mean to you?

Jerry: Well, in my instance, I started the business so I did every job.

Lynne: No, I'm talking about you with people now.

Jerry: Well, they come to me—well, I'm the boss.

Lynne: Doesn't this foster a parent–child relationship?

Jerry: No! No way. I will not tolerate that.

Lynne: How do you keep from it?

Jerry: Are you talking about a personal level or a job level?

Lynne: I'm talking about a personal-job level. The individual. Recognizing the individual as a human being having job tasks assigned to him.

Bob: That's what a father does, though. A father brings his children up to leave the nest.

Jerry: That's right. That's what I'm doing. I'm bringing them up on a personal level.

Phil: A fathering kind of thing. You can call him an adviser, a confidante.

Sue: He's the one who said "big daddy."

Jerry: Well, it's the wrong term then. I didn't mean it that way. I'm going on a personal level.

Phil: Based on the experiences he's recounting about how he developed these people. It's not a father–son relationship.

Bob: It's not a protector thing.

Sue: What do you do when somebody wants that?

Jerry: You help out. I have a supervisor and he had an eye condition. They know I have certain connections and they said, "Would you check out this doctor for me with your friends?" So I got on the phone, and it only took a five-minute phone call to get the information that this particular doctor was highly thought of in the medical community. I passed it on to the supervisor and he was very happy and indebted. So that's how I got underneath the job to a one-to-one relationship.

Lynne: But what about indebtedness?

Jerry: There's no indebtedness.

Lynne: But, you just said there was.

Jerry: I shouldn't say indebtedness. You're building that you're interested in them other than the job—as human beings. A truck is supposed to come in, and the man who puts the load on the truck doesn't put any overtime down, because the truck driver came in a half hour late. We didn't ask him not to put the overtime down. He figures he's sitting around, anyway. These are the residual things; like me making the phone call. He knows I'm interested in him, not just as a forklift driver doing a good job. I'm personally interested in how'd the operation go. I made it a point to call and find out, because he was off for the week. We move somebody and we have a potted plant waiting for the wife and kids at the new house or apartment.

Lynne: You're talking about giving strokes then, and recognition.

Jerry: People like to know that they're thought of other than the job. That they're a person.

Phil: One of the greatest motivators in the world is recognition for achievement. Recognition as a human being.

Jerry: I've sent out more potted plants for 15 bucks and I've gotten so much back. I really like them and I like to give them a feeling of a family.

Phil: It probably results in about $1500 worth of productivity.

Jerry: Oh, yeah, if you're gonna measure it, it's immeasurable. The loyalty is unbelievable.

Phil: It sounds a little manipulative.

Lynne: It is.

Jerry: But, it really isn't.

Phil: It comes from sincerity. And everything reinforces that attitude.

Jerry: If you want to look at the way I'm saying it, it really isn't. I truly like to do these things.

Phil: And there's a lot of managers that do.

Jerry: I enjoy someone saying to me, "Thanks for the plant." I enjoy that.

Lynne: You're getting something out of it.

Jerry: Of course I am. I mean because I'm getting some dollar value out of it, that's only a residual thing. There's nothing wrong with that.

Phil: You know, there's a lot of companies that don't have that luxury of being able to do that.

Jerry: I don't think that's true. You don't need a budget for that.

Bob: Authority always finds its own level.

Jerry: I've been on both sides of the street. I would like to put some entrepreneurship in a large corporation.

Bill: And that's what's motivating him. To be able to break that mold.

Jerry: That's right. That's my motivation. That's right.

Phil: So it's a challenge to you.

Jerry: That's right. That's my feeling.

Bob: Now you know what his hot button is.

Sue: I'm going to push you a little further on the question that I was asking there about people who want, who have a need for, mothering or fathering. Who seem to always be forcing you. Now we've used this term "management by objectives" or ideas that would fit into that mold and yet we've said one tool doesn't always work for everybody. Is there a way you can have two kinds of people in an organization and you can provide fathering to some people? Or do you have to just say, "No, you're better off if I don't"?

Phil: You're going to be on a spectrum of being very fatherly to being very objective and very businesslike. I will lean toward the other end of the spectrum, personally. Because my experience has been that if you attempt to be all things to all people they will thrust a dependency relationship on you. You spend a disproportionate share of your time and they never grow and everybody else gets ticked off because you're not concerned with them.

Bob: We gotta think about that individual that you're fathering or mothering and what that activity does to your whole organization. That one guy that goes and doesn't get a potted plant, what's he gonna think. You have to handle that very carefully.

Phil: One of the best things to do is to use your back-up resources. If you've got somebody that really has problems; maybe they're going through a very tough divorce or real financial problems, whatever. There are lots of organizations and agencies that are professionals in this field that can really deal with these people and do something meaningful for them. And if you try to focus on them on the job,

I've found that you're gonna typically lose; you lose their performance. And then what happens—it's very insidious; other employees will perceive what's going on. They'll want some too. And it's great to kiss and love and hug everybody, but you never get any work done that way. Somebody's gotta collect the garbage.

Lynne: I have an employee—she's been responsible for the department now for about four months. She's disorganized, she doesn't follow through, she's afraid to confront people, and I've been going through all sorts of agony trying to figure out what to do with this individual.

Phil: Eventually you'll want to replace her.

Bob: Might as well do it now.

Lynne: I have a problem within myself; I doubt that she could do the job but I'm also aware that she hasn't had the training.

Bob: Well, fulfill your obligations for training and make your judgments.

Lynne: That's what I planned on doing, and a month ago I said in one month I'm going to make a decision. Well, last week I found out that she had never had the opportunity or had not taken the opportunity to sit down and verify the job description of an employee. We ended up with a role play on how she might do this and she was so turned on it was fantastic, and the next day she was prepared for the job. But I feel like I'm holding her hand and I don't want to. A part of me doesn't want to. The other part of me would like to say, "O.K., it's cool; I'll do it for you." But I can't let myself do that.

Jerry: No, that's right. You've got to know whether to father or mother somebody—how long? And that it's not gonna be a continuing thing; we're gonna get you on your way and then you're on your own.

Bob: To me the choice of on the job and off the job—that's a tough one, too.

Phil: I can relate to what you say because the feeling may be that if you terminate that person you're saying, "Did I fail? I failed to develop that person." That's a guilt trip that you're laying on yourself. On the other hand, a person has a responsibility to grow and develop himself as well. The big problem I find with a lot of people is that they don't know what the hell their job is. Nobody ever explains it to them. And so, when you go and dump them they say, "Hey, wait a minute. Nobody ever told me what I'm supposed to really do."

Bob: Causing failures is one of the worst crimes you can perpetrate as a manager. When you overpromote or put somebody in a job without training . . .

. . .

Bob: I've invited some people up for a retreat to work over a weekend but to work on a very meaningful project that was goal oriented and company oriented, and two of the people wrote back and said, "I have other plans that weekend. Sorry." *I* would have gone to the chairman of the board's house at Lake Tahoe to work on a new venture. I would never have thought of saying "No." But it didn't bother these two people at all.

Lynne: Bob, what happened to your people that refused your invitation for the weekend?

Bob: Oh, I thought about that one a lot and . . .

Jerry: They're not with him anymore.

Bob: Actually what I did was, I pulled this off, you know, scheduled this thing with only about 10 or 14 days' notice and so I said, that is a little bit unrealistic, and they very well could have had other plans that were more important or investments made or anything, and so I wrote them back a letter and said this was a very, very important project. I understand that there were time conflicts; however, we are now scheduling it in advance and I expect there will be no conflicts at that time.

Lynne: Did you just extend an invitation the first time or did you let them know they were expected to be there?

Bob: When I say invitation it was more than that.

Phil: How did they respond?

Bob: I haven't heard back yet.

Sue: But, you see here again, we can say that our corporation expects that there's a certain amount of weekends that you're willing to give us. And I don't know how long that expectation is going to remain viable.

Phil: I suspect it will remain viable for a long time.

Lynne: But it's more acceptable today to turn down the boss's invitation.

Bob: The people who don't come, fine. They made their tradeoff.

Phil: A lot of people would perceive that kind of thing as coercion or the use of authority.

Bob: Well, they made it.

Phil: They're going to respond; they're going to react to that negatively. However, if they're given an opportunity to feel "this is a meaningful experience; we're going to talk about a new venture"—granted it's maybe over a weekend, but if the guy is really into the organization . . .

Bob: We offered a lot. I invited the husbands and wives.

three

Incentives and Rewards

OBJECTIVES

When you have completed this chapter, you should be able to:

1. Describe what a reward is and what it does.
2. Explain the importance of money as an incentive in work.
3. State an example of an activity that is intrinsically rewarding.

GLOSSARY

Intrinsic   An essential or inherent part of a thing.
Equity   That which is fair; the state in which effort and the rewards for that effort are balanced.

REWARDS

The simplest models of motivation are those which psychologists sometimes call stimulus–response models. Something happens, and an organism (any organism, perhaps a rat, or a person) responds. The response is or is not rewarded by achieving a goal, receiving a prize, finding food, or whatever. This is just as we diagrammed before:

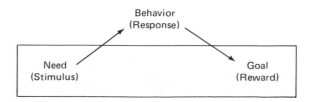

If the process is completed, it is very likely that when the stimulus recurs, the organism will reason, "The last time this happened, I behaved this way and it worked. Therefore I'll try it again." A response which achieves a goal or receives a reward is more likely to recur than one which is not rewarded. In fact we say that a person who tries an unrewarded behavior over and over is "beating his head against a stone wall," indicating that such behavior usually accomplishes nothing.

One effect of a reward is to *reinforce* or strengthen the behavior that was performed, making it more likely to occur again. Rewards are therefore important to managers, because they provide a means for encouraging desirable behaviors.

Money

In our society, the most common reward for doing work is money. Money is used most often and we are most familiar with it. It is among the rewards an organization can offer people to begin working and to do their jobs each day.

The real importance of money is difficult to determine. It is tempting to assume that it is the most important reward for work. Yet there is evidence to the contrary. We have all said at one time, "I wouldn't do that for any amount of money," or we have accepted a job which paid less than another because of some other attractive feature. Studies such as that of Herzberg, discussed in Chapter One, indicate that to many people money is not the most important thing about a job, particularly if the amount is enough to prevent *dis*satisfaction. Many firms have conducted long-term studies and have found that money is rarely ranked first in importance by employees.

Still we know that money is important for at least two good reasons. One is that money is an *instrument;* that is, it is a means for getting things people want. Money, for example, can help people fulfill their security needs by providing them with the means to get food or shelter. It might help people fulfill social needs by enabling them to join clubs, to afford social activities with other people, and to have the leisure time to enjoy such activities. Money can also serve as a *symbol;* that is, it can represent things people want. Frequently money is a symbol of a person's worth or value on the job. If a person is the highest-paid in the department, the individual may feel that his or her superiors think he or she is doing the best job. Thus money might help fulfill people's esteem needs, because it gives them information about how well they are doing and how valuable their contributions are.

This is important particularly in organizations where other information about how well a person is doing is not available. A person in a staff job may not have regular profit-and-loss reports to consult. An employee may be managed by a boss who rarely comments on work done. Often money can be a symbol for the person who is comparing his worth to that of someone doing a very different kind of work; a teacher may compare his or her salary with that of a business manager to determine the job's relative worth to society or to a specific organization.

Because of the instrumental and symbolic values of money in most western societies, sometimes we consider money a motivation in its own right. However, it is unlikely that people are born with a need for money; in many societies money is nonexistent, or at least is not very important. We consider miserly behavior (hoarding money rather than using it) unusual. It is probably more useful to think of money in terms of how it can be used rather than in an absolute sense.

Reward Systems

Organizations use many different criteria for giving rewards, which we might divide into two categories: *bio-*

graphical and *behavioral.* Biographical factors concern what a person *is*, or his life history. A salary level that is determined by the person's age, for example, or marital status is determined by biography. The ultimate reward regarding biography, of course, is a higher salary simply because a person is related to the boss! Rewards based on behavioral factors, on the other hand, are given according to what the person actually *does.* Quantity of production, value of sales made, or quality of performance would be examples. In the long run, most people seem to prefer a reward system based on performance, which also seems to get the highest productivity for the organization. However, it is not used as often as we might think, given the advantages. Consider pay based on seniority, for example. If you are paid according to the number of years you have worked in a firm, that is really a biographical basis. Obviously an extremely incompetent worker would have been fired, but seniority rewards both adequate and excellent workers the same. If employees believe that managers will be fair in their evaluations, they usually prefer performance ratings as the basis for rewards. A preference for seniority systems is voiced, on the other hand, when employees do not trust the boss to evaluate their abilities fairly.

Misuse of behavioral reward systems has led to many practices which managers might find hard to deal with. If workers feel that the work load will be increased or that they will be laid off if they produce as much as they can, they may withhold production. It they feel that the pay system is unfairly designed or operated, they may insist (through a union, for example) on pay based on predictable biographical factors such as seniority.

Most people have many needs, not just one. Thus a worker may have safety needs reflected in desires such as a guaranteed weekly wage (or hourly rate) and the use of seniority systems in determining layoffs. Yet the same person may have esteem needs which would be fulfilled more satisfactorily by a reward system which recognizes individual performance. Of course, these needs may be present in varying degrees in each worker. Typically the organization cannot tailor its pay plans to each person, so a plan is selected which satisfies most people—or so the managers assume. The plan may include a number of different reward components, but probably all of them are applied to everyone in the same ways. Very few organizations have experimented with real choices for employees, such as allowing a worker to select between finishing a quota and taking time off, or completing extra work for more pay.

Most organizations have a "mix" of rewards or incentives. As we said before, money is one of them; company benefit programs are another. However, benefit plans are generally awarded equally to all employees (or on the basis of seniority!). It would be useful to look at the kinds of rewards organizations can use for the purpose described in the first part of the chapter—to strengthen or reinforce the occurrence of some desired behavior.

Organizations can give money, of course. The basis of the piece-rate incentive plan is that the more you produce, the more you earn. Companies sometimes give bonuses to employees who perform excellently. Sales commissions are also a form of this reward. Stock options are another way of financially rewarding an employee, giving the employee a stake in the future profitability of the company. Employers assume that workers who can benefit from the company's continued prosperity will work to keep it prosperous.

Nonmonetary Rewards

Organizations have nonmonetary rewards as well. Many companies give recognition for outstanding performance with a plaque, award, or a write-up in the company newspaper. In some cases, time off or additional vacation may be given instead of money. For people with boring jobs or with strong outside interests, additional leisure time may be a very desirable reward. Too, a supervisor can give an employee praise or commendation as a reward.

Certain jobs contain inherent rewards as well. We call them "intrinsically" rewarding jobs. Many hobbies are in this category—for the hobbyist there is pleasure in doing them, but someone may do the same thing for pay! Jobs which are very important or necessary to society may be intrinsically rewarding as well. Astronauts or research scientists find their work rewarding even when the working conditions are uncomfortable or even dangerous. Pride in the workmanship or in the product also give a job intrinsic value. Some people find a job intrinsically worthwhile because they believe the organization for which they are working makes an important contribution to society.

In some cases intrinsic rewards seem to blur the distinction between work and leisure, or between vocation and avocation. Consider, for example, the clergyman or medical doctor who *is* the job because private and occupational roles are the same. Too, we might think of the research scientist who cannot imagine being anything other than a chemist; Maslow found that people fulfilling self-actualizing needs often identify with their occupations in this way. Another example might be the automobile mechanic who builds a race car during the evenings and weekends. An observer might not be able to tell whether the mechanic is performing a work or leisure activity, since the behaviors are exactly the same. In simpler societies, fewer people experience the extreme difference between work and leisure activities characteristic of industrial societies. Many people in a highly technical society perform jobs which are such a small part of a whole that they really have no separate meaning.

Researchers of on-the-job behavior have begun to think

that the importance of a reward (particularly money) is not
its size but its relationship to the work done to receive it.
This view is known as the *equity theory*. It works on the
assumption that a person who feels underpaid (or even over-
paid!) relative to someone else or to the worth of the job,
will feel uncomfortable and will act to reduce the inequity.
Thus inequity may cause behavior much like reactions to
stress which we will discuss in Chapter Four.

In experiments, researchers have made workers feel underpaid to study the resulting behavior. If a person is paid
hourly, the result is usually low output. The person is "making up for" low pay by producing only a small amount. If a
worker is paid by piece rate, however, working slowly would
only reduce the total pay. So that person is likely to produce
a high number of low-quality items. The worker compensates
by acting to raise his or her total pay in a way that does not
reward the organization (as would a large number of high-
quality items).

These experiments help to explain how people behave in
real organizations; indeed it is not uncommon for workers to
feel underpaid. These findings may help managers choose a
course of action as well. If they observe such behaviors, they
may conclude that a real pay inequity exists and may take
the initiative to correct it. If such action is not possible or
if the problem is in the employee's understanding, the
manager may try to publicize or clarify the pay structure, or
devise more nonmonetary rewards.

META-GOALS

Armed with the concepts of "self-actualization" from Maslow's model in Chapter One and "intrinsic rewards" from this
chapter, we can now consider a topic which will be mentioned throughout the Winthrop Management Series; that

is, the idea of *meta-goals,* or overall ideals which are important to a person. Most people have causes or ideals for which they are willing to work very hard, even if it requires personal sacrifice or inconvenience. Their actions with respect to such goals represent needs which arc higher up on the need hierarchy. We may also assume that work toward such goals is intrinsically rewarding.

Meta-goals include many things that people desire. We may wish to advance the cause of a nation, a religion, or an ethnic group. We may desire to support some change in social or economic conditions. Or meta-goals may be closer to home. In any case, they transcend or override other goals so that we are willing to sacrifice for them and feel greatly rewarded by working toward them, even if it is unlikely that we will see their eventual fulfillment.

In some cases, people may be employed by organizations which are directly involved with their personal meta-goals: a church, a political party, or the United Nations. We would expect that these people would find their jobs intrinsically rewarding, even if the particular jobs are simple or repetitious. It is more likely, as was suggested earlier, that most people in our society are not directly employed by organizations which work toward their meta-goals. Therefore many volunteer behaviors may be exhibited by such people. Some organizations attempt to promote volunteer work by providing time off or leaves of absence for people to work on socially important projects. Thus the organization recognizes the existence of such goals and provides opportunities to fulfill them as rewards.

USING REWARDS

When a foreman or supervisor asks, "How do I motivate my employees?" the first answer usually is related to incentives and rewards. We motivate employees (or more accurately, channel the motivations which they already have to action) by rewarding or reinforcing those actions which are desirable from the organization's point of view. A manager may cause workers to behave in the first place by training them or showing them what to do. Or we may use influence by one of the methods discussed in Chapter Two. Then when we get the behavior we want, we reward it.

How to reward behavior is not easy to determine. There are at least two things to consider. One concerns what rewards are available to use. A first-line supervisor may rely heavily on praise, commendations, recommendation for promotion, and the like—he may not be able to recommend people for the company stock-option plan, and so could not use that as a reward even if it existed. The other consideration is the employee to be rewarded. Some employees want extra work and would see an overtime assignment as a reward —other employees might consider it a punishment! These two considerations illustrate that there is no easy rule to tell a supervisor how to reward employees. The supervisor must look at the individual employees and at the kinds of rewards that are available to offer.

The supervisor must use both creativity and realism in selecting rewards for employees. Lower-level supervisors and managers in nonprofit organizations such as schools or government agencies, sometimes are discouraged when they realize the great array of profit-oriented rewards available at higher levels in profit-making firms. But the job of management cannot be done by wishing for unavailable reward systems. The manager must be realistic about the options and also creative in recognizing and using the possible rewards.

One additional clue can be derived from the motivational models discussed in Chapter One. If the manager understands the needs of workers, the individual will be more able to predict which rewards will mean most to them. Once again, being able to recognize the needs of others is a very important skill.

SUMMARY

Rewards or incentives reinforce behavior; they make it more likely that the behavior will recur. In our society, one of the most common incentives is money, but organizations offer many other intangible rewards as well. Rewards are most effective when they are directly related to behavior, rather than biographical factors, such as a person's age. Rewards are an important answer to the question, "How can I motivate employees?"

SKILL DEVELOPERS

1. List all the rewards or incentives available for you to give to the people you manage. Think of one particular person who would be "turned on" by each. If you can, think of a person who might be neutral to or even "turned off" by each.
2. Think of four or five instances when you have felt really rewarded by someone or something. What was the reward in each case?
3. Choose someone you know whose behavior you want to change or strengthen. Can you do so by rewarding the desired behavior by some means available to you?

REFERENCES

OPSAHL, ROBERT L., AND DUNNETTE, MARVIN. "The Role of Financial Compensation in Industrial Motivation." *Psychological Bulletin* 66 (1966):94-118.

PANEL DISCUSSION

In this section, the panelists discuss the mix of incentives available to them and how people vary in their responses to different reward systems.

Sue: I suspect Lynne is now getting at something I wanted to talk about earlier, and that is about specific incentives. Is going to Tahoe to water ski an incentive you can offer in your setting? It's not one that my boss can, but it may be one that you can offer, because of the setting of your organization.

Bob: My judgment is, play your best shot.

Sue: That's one half of it; what are some of the ranges of this smorgasbord you talked about earlier? But the other is, which of the incentives are really incentives to the people to whom they are being offered?

Bob: You have to know your audience.

Sue: We have for any given setting a range of incentives that are available to us. Over there we have a group of people and "know your audience" is perhaps a compact way of saying something I'd like to see us expand on a little. What are the ranges of alternatives and how do we find out which ones fit which people?

Jerry: You've got to know your audience. That means you get to know on a one-to-one basis before you can find out what the common denominator is.

Phil: There's another condition I think in Bob's case. If he is having a meeting that plans something, a new venture or whatever it might be, it seems to me the real incentive to be at that meeting is, in fact, achievement.

Jerry: You're a part of that venture.

Bob: It's a chance to create.

Phil: All the things. Creativity, achievement, growth, responsibility, being in on things. That's the real incentive. Now the
other things are maybe some window dressing. By the way,
we're going to be in Tahoe; there will be some speedboats . . .

Bob: "How do we accomplish this goal with the most fun?"

Phil: You've gotta be honest with people; you've gotta really
level with them. "Hey, this is a crappy job, and the best
thing about it is it pays 6 bucks an hour; and you can make
a lot of overtime."

Bob: We face that a lot in the food business. How do you get
people to peel potatoes and say, "Now, that's it"? On the
one hand we will get a full-time person, that is their life
and on the other hand we will get a college student as a way
of working his way through college. You get in and say,
"You are a salad person, you peel potatoes and carrots and
you're going to get your $2.50 an hour and you get all those
things, but that's it." You've got to work with them and say,
"Now if you want to learn something else, I will put you on
as an assistant cook, two hours every evening." And consequently you get a job that is, for years, and probably in the
future will be, too, 40 to 60 percent turnover. And that becomes a fact of life for the manager. It means his job is to
accept and learn to live with it. Because those people come
and go and I don't blame them. It is just a bad job. So they've
got to go out of your walls to get better.

Phil: It's interesting because you probably see a more highly
educated level of people taking some of these less responsible jobs because of the economic climate right now. You
know, you hear about Ph.D.'s and masters' degree holders
that are willing to take virtually any job—pumping gas, bag-

ging groceries, because it's a bloody job. And the motivation of these kinds of people, I think, is a difficult process.

Bob: It's almost untouchable, because they see that only as transitory. And they take this job and "I'm not a dishwasher because I am an engineer."

Lynne: But if you can accept that, as a manager, you know that they're only going to be there for a short period of time, they can fulfill your needs and you can fulfill some of theirs.

Bob: But then you treat them as though that's a transitory job and you treat them as though they are better than they are. And you both find yourselves in a difficult situation, let's both make the best of it. Again, it's getting it out front early.

Phil: My first job when I came out of the service was interviewing people for assembly jobs and the pay was, like, $2 an hour. A lot of college people would come in for jobs. What I'd try to do is to say, "Here's the work—it's monotonous, it's dull, it's hot, it's sweaty, it's 40 hours. You get a 10-minute break in the morning, a 10-minute break in the afternoon, half an hour for lunch—do you really want it?" If a guy really could say, "Well, yeah, I really need a job," then you'd get into a better evaluation of the individual. Is he right for it or is he not? But to me, companies make a great mistake when they do not level with potential employees very early in the game, because they tend to oversell jobs. People get very antagonistic about that. They're sold a bill of goods. And let's face it—there are jobs in the industries that we have that you can't automate. They're basically low-paying, rather menial jobs, but they're essential jobs.

Bob: The only thing that frustrates me—you're talking about motivation and this is kind of my bag—is that when you take unemployment insurance and all these other things, you've got to be paying that group of people that would be taking those jobs 90 percent of what they could get by doing these cruddy jobs. What are we doing to those people who get something for nothing virtually? And we take that pool of resources away form the work society. That really puts us all in a bad place, I think.

Sue: I think that we've seen the emergence of a group of young people, particularly—and perhaps this relates back to what you were saying, too, coming to a company and being willing to take a subsistence-level work, of people willing to take more transitory jobs. We seem to have emerged with some sort of younger subgroup who says, "I don't want a job for the challenge; I want it for the pay, and I'll quit it as soon as I have enough money and go spend 6 months on a motorcycle, and then maybe I'll come back."

Phil: I don't think that phenomenon is necessarily limited to young people, either. I think you're seeing the same thing among people in their—over 30—I mean—you know, the over-the-hill gang.

Lynne: Over 40, even.

Phil: I had an interesting luncheon the other day. I was with a group of very young people—I would say they were in their early twenties, and, you know, we were kind of rapping about work and the substance of jobs and responsibility and the enrichment aspect and they were very, very oriented toward dollars, and work itself was secondary. I'm not saying that's a generalization for all young people—but it doesn't seem to me that we can make the broad generalization that, say, young people are only interested in enriching work. I think very often they are very concerned about the dollar aspects of the jobs, the rewards involved—just as much as I ever was.

Sue: Well, Bob, you—I'd like to get back a little bit to a contrast I've thought about in relation to some of the food service work—that there must be times when you have career potato peelers and college part-time potato peelers standing next to each other with somebody trying to manage both of them.

Bob: You deal with each one differently. That part-timer, that student, he sees himself as that. He is a student and he's taking history courses and biology and so forth and he's peeling potatoes four hours a week just for spending money. No problem. You talk to him about his classes or this kind of thing, and treat him as a student. The real problem comes with that full-time potato peeler who sees himself or herself caught there, and seeing the student is gonna be able to get away from it and get a bigger and better life. And you've gotta deal with that person another way.

Phil: I think there's an analogy between that and the service. Now, for example, the young second lieutenants are going through basic training—you know, the sergeants are involved in teaching. The sergeant's been a master sergeant for fifteen years or so and this guy's going to be a second lieutenant in 90 days. You know. "And he's going to tell me how to run my company, or my battalion?"

Bob: "Because he wears gold on his shoulders, he is better than I am and more knowledgeable? No way."

Jerry: And there's a resentment within management, especially with the educated versus the uneducated—and there's a feeling of inferiority, and you try to tell them they can take courses, but there's still that—he knows more about how to run a plant than the man on the street. Even after a year, he's going to look like the analogy of the sergeant versus the 90-day wonder. And this is a bridge that the 90-day wonder and the college graduate are going to have to overcome.

Bob: You know, I find that when you tell that person that you started at that low job and brought him up, you can help yourself, you can go to school—they're afraid of school; they're afraid of college. And I almost feel guilty about that and then you really get frustration and. . . . That's misusing motivation in some cases.

Jerry: That's right, and so I don't press it. There are several ways you motivate people if you don't have the money. I pulled something onto one of my supervisors. He was a Cuban who couldn't live under the Castro regime, and I had great success with him. I gave him a language course, voluntarily, and I think it cost me 300 bucks. It was a cassette; you didn't have to go to school; he did it at home in his own environment and perhaps his wife was able to get a residual effect from it. This was a subtle way of telling them that we had hopes for them and that he had a place to go in this organization, and that he had the mentality and the ability. All he had as a problem was communication in another language.

Bob: You know, what's neat about that is that you were helping him off-site, too. That language thing will help him away from work, at work . . .

Jerry: Right, right. He was aware that he wasn't married to the company, but I think there is an obligation on his part. He would feel that, "Well, after all he did give me this and I should do this." And, so, it's worked out; but there's different techniques. But I think it's gotta be definite, on a one-to-one basis. You can't get it out of the textbook. There's no one generalization—"Use this and it's going to work." It doesn't happen. There's too many different things out there in society that people like.

Lynne: I was thinking about something that Bob was talking about with potato peelers. I think there's another small element that are very content to be potato peelers, and they don't want any additional responsibility. They'd like to be left alone. You come in and try job enrichment and they say, "My God, would you go back and leave me alone? I know my job."

Phil: "Would you mind if I don't do this?" You know?

Lynne: "I don't want you to change it. I like it."

Jerry: Well, that's where the manager comes in and where he has to pick the shot. And thank God for people like that. Because there's always going to be those menial jobs. And as long as they take pride and do their menial job, you're home free. Well, why push it?

Phil: Yeah, there's an interesting book about the very same thing you've been talking about called *Working* by Studs Terkel. I think it's a great textbook for anybody in any career. He interviews a cross-section of people from waitresses to roustabouts to hookers to stewardesses to stenographers to salesmen, managers, virtually any walk of life. And the message that comes through is, "Gee, we've lost our sense of craftsmanship in the job." He singled out a couple of heroes in the book, and one of them was—I think it was a truck-driver or something like that. He was going to drive that rig better than it had ever been driven before. And the waitress who said, "Gee, there's a certain technique to getting that plate to that guy in the right way to make him feel good." And it suddenly came back, "There's a sense of pride in even the dullest jobs—even the dullest jobs." I have a tendency to put people down because they like it. Now wait a minute —what's wrong with that kind of work? They've got work that's honorable; it may not pay as much as you might like, but there's a real sense of satisfaction out of doing a good job. And it's too bad that we've engineered a lot of it out.

Jerry: Because a man feels he's got tenure, he's protected. If he does a crappy job or what have you, you've gotta write him up before you're able to demote him or to get him out of the front door. We find this with some of our people who are up for the foreman ladder who are really good people in the lower echelon and are actually good people the first year or two as a foreman. Then they become complacent. They just don't give a damn. 'Cause, what the hell? No matter how tough things get, "I've got ten, twelve years. You can't drop me." And they goof up and they make all sorts of mistakes and it's very frustrating.

Lynne: I don't think the union's going to come back on management if management is truly trying to get that employee involved. We've managed to develop a good relationship with the reps from the union and this wasn't the case four or five years ago.

Jerry: Yeah, but I think, Lynne, in all fairness, when you're dealing with human lives—I mean, if a guy gives a patient a wrong pill, it could be fairly . . .

Lynne: I'm not dealing with the professional person, I'm dealing with clerks. The nurse is the only one that's giving the medication. I'm talking about the employee that's fallen off, that just doesn't give a damn anymore. I've had some experience with our union, and the majority of the time they're all for helping that individual come alive again. If they're turned off all they're going to do is bellyache to the union anyway.

Phil: I think we have a tendency to judge other people by their behavior while we judge ourselves by our intentions. And sometimes we impute to other organizations the wrong kinds of intentions. I've had that problem sometimes in dealing with unions. It's always the same old bit; all I want is money, money, more time off. They may really be interested in making that job a little bit more interesting.

Jerry: Basically, union agents are people within the craft who were voted by their popularity; they're good politicians and they become representative of the union. They're not unsophisticated, but they don't have the background in negotiation. They only know that they want more. Here's another interesting phenomenon. In the baking industry we have, because of cost and what have you, had to automate. So everybody working in my operation is really not a baker, all he's got to do is turn an on-off switch and follow directions.

Phil: He's a machine operator.

Jerry: Right. Well, the union agent is an ex-baker who made the dough by hand and he had to sponge it, and he had to feel it, so it was an art. What we've done is taken an art and turned it into a science. So there's a certain amount of resentment. Here this punk kid comes in and turns the switch on and he's got eight bucks an hour. It took me 16 years— 6 years to work behind an old German baker who taught me, beat the hell out of me for 18 hours a day for 25¢ an hour, and this kid's making more money and he still doesn't know how to make it right. So the resentment there is for the old versus the new. And we can't use any old time laborers on an operation because they just don't know how to handle the equipment. They don't have the skill.

Sue: I'd like to look a little more at this old and the new and maybe talk a little about the particular problems of the younger people skipping over older people and if that doesn't make a particular problem in motivating people. You may have people who work for you who are younger than you are or who have been around longer or . . .

Bob: I'll tell you one thing. In my opinion, the young people are turned off by promotions by seniority. You need a system of promotion and it's not just done on seniority, and without that you will not attract a whole bunch of young people.

Jerry: This is a very serious problem that we have with unions, where seniority is the criterion in job bidding. Very serious.

Bob: One motivational plug out of your chess game right there.

Jerry: And if you want to bring up another problem thanks to the government—no offense—is the E.O.C. with the women—equal opportunities—has created a tremendous problem for me personally.

Bob: I was afraid we were going to get into that.

Sue: It seems to me we're talking about two motivational difficulties here—one of them is a group of people, whether it be racial minorities or females, who come into an organization socialized with experiences much different from other people in the organization, having never worked before or not having worked at those sorts of jobs, and the organization not understanding how to motivate them. The other is the feelings of the people upon whom they are brought in. They're saying, as you said, "I spent 16 years learning how to do this and here's this kid that the boss tells me he's got to hire." Have you had any of this sort of experience? Having to bring in new kinds of people?

Lynne: We have a lot of entry-level people. And it seems as though many of the new hires are more geared to go up the ladder, their merit and ability actually scaled out higher than the individual who's been there for a long while. Now perhaps the individual who's been there at the entry-level position doesn't want to move on. We always have that person who feels they should be given the better job at the top, and they're really not equipped for it. They do resent the kid who comes in and really has it together, the one who is qualified to go on.

Phil: That is probably one of the most difficult supervisor-management problems you ever encounter, because you want to retain the goodwill and services of that other employee because you pay him for that. What you really pay for is performance, yet you want to develop that leader or that superstar performer. How do you do one without alienating the other or wrongfully expending your time to the detriment of the other? It's rough.

Bob: Many times that good person who's been there a long time is not motivated for promotion. He blocks one of the ladder steps and you've got to get that young climber into that position for only six months or something.

Jerry: I've found that the only way especially with an old employee, you have to sit him down and be honest with him and say, "In my opinion, I think you've reached your plateau."

Phil: That's gutsy management, I think, on your part. Because what you've finally recognized is that the guy's reached his limited growth potential. And you're really leveling with the guy. It's tough.

Bob: And 80 percent of the time they know it themselves. It's just not possible for them to admit it.

Jerry: Nobody wants to admit it. Nobody likes to be told they're limited in their ability; even though they know it's true; they don't want to hear it.

Phil: That is really biting the bullet, 'cause what happens if you don't do that, if you ever have to have a layoff or termination? We always think about industry as growing, well it's not—and you lay off that old star performer, and you've given him reviews that say, "This guy is great. We love him, you know. His sibling rivalries are great, no psychosexual hangups. Beautiful." And all of a sudden, "Hey, I'm laid off. Well, I thought my ratings say I'm great."

Lynne: "You've told me how fantastic I am all these years and now what are you doing?"

Bob: Your actions speak more loudly than your words.

Jerry: If that's not the spirit of the organization, then everybody feels insecure.

Phil: But, on the other hand, let's face it, you've got to terminate people. You really have to be a bastard and terminate somebody and they don't like it. But very often you grow as a result of that because your organization says, "He finally booted out that bug." Because they know who the marginal performers are.

Lynne: I think, on the other hand, when you're talking about the kid who's come into the organization, and is encouraged to get ahead, you also have the obligation to be very honest with him. To tell him when he's coming on too strong, and really stepping out of line, rather than just letting him go. It takes a lot of time and counseling.

Jerry: Well, I'll tell you, the other people will usually step on him pretty good. They're waiting for him. They know how to —they know how to get their shots in.

Lynne: You can turn him loose to the wolves.

Jerry: Well, he's got to survive in that jungle. You can't protect him.

Lynne: I think you owe him a certain amount of counseling and guidance. If he still wants to go ahead and stick his neck out, let him go.

Jerry: Right now I'm interviewing an assistant. And I told him, "The first few months are the roughest. We're going to see how the new boy on the street's going to work and we're going to chop you up. You'd better low-key it. Now, do it any way you want. I'll be there right behind you. All I can do is put a Band-aid on you. I can't protect you that much 'cause you're going to be out there alone."

Phil: You're doing it before you even hire the guy. He knows what he's getting into first. It's his choice. His expectations are realistic.

Jerry: That's right. I mean I want to lay it all out. I think you're painting a much blacker picture than it is. And if he's willing to accept it, then don't come back and say you didn't tell me something. I'm also doing it for my own protection.

Phil: It's expensive to hire and train a person.

Bob: It's a good thing to do with this young tiger that's just joined the organization. It's realistic to say the first promotion will probably be three to five years out.

Lynne: I wish somebody had told me that.

Bob: If you can go to bed with that and be at peace with it, then you're off to a good start.

Sue: I'd like to go more deeply into something we've been touching on; how people like to be managed, or how people like to be influenced. We've said, "Nobody likes to hear bad things about themselves," but then we've said, "Everybody wants to hear the bad things about themselves."

Jerry: I don't think it's bad things.

Bob: We said realistic things.

Phil: As close to the truth . . .

Jerry: Objectivity, right.

Phil. People know it themselves. For example, my first review the guy told me everything I knew about myself. It was the things I tried to hide; for example, "Phil, you don't follow through on details." I know I don't follow through on details. "Phil, you have a tendency to burn out rather quickly." I know that. But, at least, it put down and quantified for me a target to work on.

Jerry: And you had to respect the man. You didn't put anything over on him.

Phil: Otherwise the review sounds completely different. "Phil, you did a fantastic job; you're beautiful." "Don't I do anything wrong?" "Gee, Phil, no. Let's not talk about that." O.K., but the guy doesn't grow as a result. And I think that, really, the way people grow—it sounds negative —is sometimes a bad experience. Getting fired somewhere along in their career.

Jerry: It's a very healthy thing.

Lynne: You're saying be honest with people.

Phil: I think it's imperative to do that. A lot of people can't handle it. They don't like it. But, to me the price you pay down the stream is much greater, you know, because you lose performance; and you create a human relations problem where you're spending a disproportionate share of your time managing one or two individuals. And I think the studies tend to show that in sales. Eighty percent of the sales manager's job is spent dealing with 20 percent of his people. The other 80 percent is pretty well squared away.

Bob: You said something there I'm not sure I agree with. I think people learn most by their pinnacle experience; be it success or failure. And I think you've got to allow at any job a place for those experiences to happen. You've got to be able to fail or you've got to be able to be really big. From that will people learn. They don't learn from the hum-drum type thing.

Lynne: That would imply not protecting the people on either end, I guess. That implies honesty both in saying, "That really was a fantastic job," and in saying, "Sorry, but you're out the door."

Bob: Jerry said it when we started. It gives them enough rope to go on that they can do those things. It's there— that they can go pretty darn far.

Jerry: I've told people they've done a fantastic job, but that they did it the hard way. I've corrected the job done even though they've obtained the goal. I've said all this spinning the wheels that you've done, where, if you'd done it this way . . . I'm not saying that you haven't done a good job; you've got the goal, but you had to come down on Saturdays and Sundays; you worked for 14 weeks solid, 10 days a week. Now that's not necessary. If I was doing it, I would do it in such a way . . . and look at all the time you could have saved. Now, the next time this comes up do it any way you want, but you have an alternative. You don't have to repeat what you did as long as you attain the goal. And then it's their decision.

. . .

Sue: Let me ask a couple of things that I kind of would like to have available on the tape. One of them is what incentives, what rewards, do you like to use most? If you could reach into that bag and pull out what you really think is the one that works—there'd be more bucks or your name in the company paper or what?

Bob: Yeah, I think recognition. Peer acceptance, that kind of thing. One of the best. You can do it at the right time. You can always do it at the right time.

Phil: I think it's a coordinated effort really. I think if you are a participating type of manager you're going to use a lot of different incentives in your bag of tricks. You might, for example, want to give more responsibility. That to me is the best way, because it does provide for individual growth. Concomitant with that would be achievement, responsibility, as Bob points out, recognition both formal and informal, delegation; to me you can harmonize and orchestrate all these. That's a powerful incentive. That's recognition.

Sue: How much do you rely on a formal organization's incentives—the bag they've created?

Jerry: Use it as a tool. You don't rely on it because every organization's slightly different. But you try to be cohesive and work it in.

Phil: Sometimes you get a very highly structured organization, for example, your pay policies are such that you only grant increases at certain times, at certain percentage increments; you're limited so you've got to be really creative.

Bob: It's kind of a "given," you manage within that box.

Phil: The parameters of what you can do.

Jerry: It depends on the level you're talking about, but if the guy's up there on management level and he's done a good job you call him in, and you tell him, "You did a fantastic job. Just wanted to let you know. We really appreciate it and you're doing great."

Bob: Then you write your boss a letter about him.

Jerry: And he gets a copy of the letter.

Sue: Well, let's go down a level then and ask if that same strategy works if you're talking about the guy out there on the line?

Jerry: Well you can give him the goodies, you know, you give him a day off with pay or you can give him a raise or you can promote him.

Bob: Or right in front of his peers you walk up to him and say, "Hey, today's your anniversary."

Jerry: Then you write him a letter and then you send it to him at his home so he can show it to his wife and kids. Put his picture in the company organ or you put a notice up on the bulletin board. He made a suggestion and not only is he getting $50.00, but he's made the job easier, or thanks to him—you know—the lunch room is clean. Now we get fresh sandwiches. Now we have hot coffee, now we get brewed coffee instead of instant coffee. It's again recognition, and then again you play where he'll get the most out of it. Where the individual feels like something. He feels that he's been recognized.

Bob: You should always go to that person before you do something. "I would like to put your picture in the company paper."

Jerry: Check with him.

Lynne: I don't think those goodies are the most effective way. Picture in the paper, the trophy, and all these things, or the plant from the boss. I think that the day-to-day coaching must come first to give the strokes when they are actually deserved—that's much more important and effective.

Jerry: In other words, you're not a son-of-a-bitch all year round and two days a year you're a nice guy. That doesn't work.

Sue: Lynne, that reminds me of something. Will you define "strokes" so we can get that on the tape. I'd like to have you say it, so that we can have it in your own words.

Lynne: I'm talking about positive feedback, and the recognition for doing something that's certainly acceptable if not outstanding.

Phil: Acknowledgment.

four

Punishments and Stress

OBJECTIVES

When you have completed this chapter, you should be able to:

1. Explain what punishment is, and how it differs from reward.
2. Describe the reactions to stress.
3. Understand how stress spurs people to action.

GLOSSARY

Discipline Training which is intended to correct or improve behavior. Sometimes the term is also used to mean punishment intended to correct behavior.

PUNISHMENT

In Chapter Three we discussed rewards, factors that increase the probability of a behavior being repeated. We might expect punishments to be factors that decrease the probability of a behavior being repeated. However, punishments are somewhat more complicated than that.

One of the primary drives introduced in Chapter One is the avoidance of pain. It differs from other drives because it concerns escaping from something rather than getting something. There are punishments related to this drive, and organisms, whether they are animals or people, can learn certain behaviors or avoid others in order to avoid pain. But in fact, most punishments are not directly related to pain. Even spanking a child has components other than physical pain. These components probably have more effect than the physical act of the spanking.

As we grow, we learn additional motivations. We learn that some things are threatening—to the fulfillment of our needs, or to our self-image (our picture of ourselves). So we learn to avoid those threats. We try to do an acceptable job at work to avoid being fired (which would jeopardize security), or to avoid being bawled out by the boss (which would be embarrassing and weaken our self-image). Accordingly we may assume that the need to avoid these threats reduces the likelihood of poor work behavior.

However, punishment does not necessarily change behavior. Washing a child's mouth out with soap may prevent the child from saying certain words in a parent's presence, but it probably will not stop this behavior in other settings. Punishment, in other words, may cause the punished person to conceal certain behavior from whoever punished him. However, psychologists now believe that punishment does not eliminate undesirable behavior entirely. It seems that undesirable behavior is eliminated by lack of reward rather than by punishment. We may conclude that a repeated behavior is rewarded consistently. If we want to eliminate undesirable behavior we must discover the reward the misbehaver receives and eliminate it.

Therefore we can only expect to *suppress* behavior by punishment, but not necessarily to alter it or to eliminate its undesirable aspects. It provides still another clue to the question, "How do I motivate employees?" Punishment is not really a motivator of desired behavior. At best, it can only help suppress undesired behavior. In order to banish an undesirable behavior completely, we must look at the situation and eliminate the rewards for that behavior. If an employee does careless work, the person may feel he or she is "getting back at" a supervisor or that resulting customer complaints may reflect badly on someone the worker does not like. It is probably more important to remove the reward than to institute a punishment.

On the other hand, suppose an employee is doing a good, commendable job. If the worker is not rewarded, there is nothing to reinforce that behavior. Failure to reward may result in the loss of desirable behaviors! Therefore it pays to reinforce the behavior we want so that it will continue.

However, sometimes a manager only wants to suppress an employee's undesirable behavior, not extinguish it entirely. For example, consider the drinking of alcoholic beverages. A manager may not wish to regulate an employee's behavior outside the work setting, but may use punishment (or the threat of punishment) to suppress this behavior at work. The manager could make rules against drinking on the job or coming to work intoxicated. Of course, a further complication may arise if the employee responds by drinking in secret at work, rather than drinking after work only. Obviously punishment does not always work the way it is intended.

Discipline in Organizations

All organizations have rules. There are certain behaviors they want all members to perform (for example, punching a time clock) and others they wish to forbid. In order to enforce these rules, organizations use the influence methods previously discussed as well as reward and punishment. The intent is to discipline employees and train them to behave according to company regulations.

In some small organizations, as in a family, discipline may be relatively informal and on a personal level. A certain behavior may be punished in one instance and ignored the next, or punished severely by one person and lightly by another.

It may be that such inconsistency interferes with the corrective effect of discipline. For this reason, an organization may decide that disciplinary measures should be uniform throughout and develop a disciplinary system. Typically, the system would spell out what actions are punishable and what the punishments will be.

Disciplinary systems may be instituted as a result of pressures from sources other than the organization's managers. A union may demand a formal system to prevent arbitrary or unfair punishments. Or, a government agency may call for such a system as proof that there is no discriminatory use of punishment against particular individuals or groups. Whatever the reason for their development, disciplinary systems in organizations are very common. We can hardly imagine life without them. Many organizations have very formal and complicated hierarchies of disciplinary measures, ranging from verbal reprimands through written reprimands and pay-docking, to disciplinary layoffs and firing.

Of course these systems do not always solve all the problems for which they were designed. Employees may figure out ways to "get around" the system, or supervisors may be arbitrary in their punishments despite the rules. Too, another kind of problem may arise from a uniform and inflexible system. In the informal system of the small company the supervisor could "tailor" a disciplinary measure to a particular person or incident. Under a formal system, he or she must use the same disciplinary measure without question even if the effect on the offender will be much different. One employee may not be bothered at all by a written reprimand, for example, while another may be deeply distressed. Or a punishable act (such as tardiness) may seem to the employee to have been beyond his or her control, and thus the discipline imposed will seem unfair even though the rules state that it is correct.

Some companies have eliminated disciplinary procedures

as an experiment. Most have been pleased with the results. Of course they had to reserve the right to "separate" the rare misfit employee. However, these companies performed better than they had expected with less stringent systems of discipline. Obviously not every company could do this. Size, type of work, and labor-management relations affect the ability of a firm to eliminate disciplinary procedures. However, as more data regarding the cost of such programs versus their effectiveness are compiled, it is possible that more organizations will change their policies.

STRESS

There are unpleasant things other than punishment which we learn to avoid as well. We call some of these factors *stress*. Stress is part of the motivational process and is related to the actions we take to reach a goal. When something goes wrong with this process, we experience stress. We will consider three kinds of stress—frustration, anxiety, and conflict. Each comes from a different kind of obstacle to goal achievement.

Frustration

A *frustration* is something which prevents a person from reaching a goal; that is, the person is "blocked" from behaving in a certain way to achieve the goal. If you want to drive to work in the morning but your car will not start, you are frustrated in your attempt. In our diagram, it would appear as:

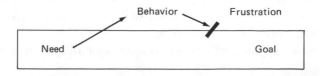

How do people react when they are frustrated? Consider the automobile example. You might feel like kicking the car or shouting at it; or you might call road service or take the bus. These reactions illustrate the general categories of responses to stress. The first is releasing feelings about the frustration—we may act aggressively (kick the car), defensively ("I didn't do it, don't blame me"), or protectively ("I didn't really want to go to work after all"). The other is choosing some alternative behavior to reach the goal. Generally the choice between the two categories of response is not a conscious one. A person's reaction usually depends on his or her picture of the situation. If the "block" is really not the fault of the individual, such as a flat tire, usually the person will not feel threatened. However, if the "block" threatens a person's self-image (instills a feeling of incompetence or guilt), the individual often will react defensively. It is hard to predict the reaction, unless you know how the person sees the block. Obviously it is more constructive for the person to find a way around the difficulty by some alternative behavior.

We have mentioned previously that discomfort (physiological discomfort in Chapter One, inequity in Chapter Three) causes people to act in order to reduce the discomfort. This is true of stress as well. In the example of frustration, the person experiencing the block is uncomfortable and acts to reduce his or her discomfort. This fact can be very useful. First we can use it to diagnose what is wrong. A person behaving defensively is often experiencing frustration. Too, we can use it to help choose corrective action. Perhaps through advice or training, the person can learn to overcome the block. Also, it may be possible to design the situation in another way so that it is not as frustrating. Possibly the threatening aspect of the frustration can be removed even if the block still exists.

You probably know people you think of as defensive. They seem more concerned with protecting themselves than with correcting the difficulty. Often people learn to behave that way if they have had many punitive experiences. Managers can avoid developing defensive employees by adopting a problem-solving approach rather than a blaming one. Often the organization will benefit more by solving the problem than by pinning the blame on someone. This is related to the collaborative method of influence. We may get better results if we say, "We have a problem—let's try to correct it," rather than, "Whose fault is it?"

In a work setting some frustration is unavoidable. Individuals and the organizations they work for may have goals which cannot be attained at the same time. People do not leave their needs at home, even though they cannot be fulfilled on the job. An effective manager helps motivate employees by reducing frustration whenever possible, by eliminating threatening situations, and by identifying alternative courses of action.

Anxiety

Anxiety is a stress also related to frustration. However, instead of being a reaction to past or present occurrences, anxiety involves looking toward the future. When a person is concerned with or threatened by the possibility of future frustration, that individual is experiencing anxiety. Since no one can predict the future perfectly, there will always be uncertainty about what is going to happen and therefore always some anxiety. In fact this may be beneficial. Mild anxiety can act as a motivating force; this is the reaction athletes feel before competing. Their senses are sharper and they are more active. They are "up" for the game. Mild anxiety, which results from not knowing exactly what is going to happen, can cause people to behave more efficiently or more creatively.

However, the effects of greater anxiety can be detrimental. People suffering from moderate anxiety often are so uncertain about the future that instead of looking forward to it they become fearful and overly cautious. Rather than trying new things, they fall back on "safe" behaviors or habits. Such people often want an authority figure to tell them what to do. Severe anxiety is the most deteriorating. People suffering from it may experience breakdowns in their customary behavior patterns and often cannot distinguish safe from harmful situations. They assume they must be afraid of everything. Usually people experiencing extreme anxiety are not found in the work setting except where there is danger or a threat to their security.

If mild anxiety is helpful and moderate and severe anxiety are undesirable, we should want to control the amount of anxiety people feel. This is difficult because each person experiences a different level of anxiety in any given situation. Phobias illustrate this difference. A person who is afraid to fly may experience severe anxiety in an airplane while a skydiver would find the setting exciting and stimulating. A retail store manager might set quotas for sales clerks, only to find that some of them enjoyed trying to meet them while other clerks became depressed or frightened. Students often have a similar problem. A quiz or test challenges some students and as a result they perform well. Others experience "test anxiety"; the test situation is so stressful that they freeze and are unable to perform.

We noted that people act to reduce discomfort, for example in response to frustration. People also act to reduce anxiety because of the discomfort of anxiety. Knowing this is useful to the manager. When he or she observes rigid or stereotyped behavior, it should be a clue that something is causing an undesirable level of anxiety. The level may be reduced by providing more information about the future, or by clarifying what the consequences of various behaviors are. For example, a manager may discuss company plans for expansion with employees if they are concerned about potential changes, or reassure a nervous new employee that one mistake does not mean he or she will be fired. The manager has a double challenge. The person must not create an atmosphere which is so routine or repetitious that it is totally predictable (no uncertainty). On the other hand, the level of anxiety of employees should not reach a point where desirable reactions are stifled and undesirable behavior replaces them.

One problem related to anxiety which managers often face is resistance to change. Indeed the manager's job is to make his or her department "more" something—more efficient, more effective, more productive. In order to do this, often the manager must introduce changes. If you have ever been in this situation, you may have been surprised and disappointed that employees tried to prevent the changes from occurring, or if they were instituted, from being successful. Anxiety is a major reason why employees resist change. They do not know the consequences of the change so they assume that the change is threatening. A solution to the problem can be found in the concept of participation mentioned in Chapter Two. If employees feel they are part of the decision-making process which results in a change, they are less apt to feel threatened by the change. This idea will be discussed further in Chapter Five.

Conflict

The final kind of stress we will consider occurs when we have to make choices or decisions. We call this kind of stress *conflict*. Conflict may occur when there are different behaviors possible to reach a goal or when a person must choose between goals (see the accompanying illustration).

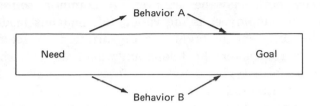

In fact conflict can occur whenever a person has two or more ideas or pieces of information which do not agree. Conflict also acts as a motivating force—a person experiencing conflict is uncomfortable and wants to change the conditions of the situation in order to reduce the discomfort.

It is possible to reduce the discomfort created by conflict in a number of ways. If the conflict results from the need to choose between behaviors or between goals, sometimes making a choice reduces the discomfort. (However, afterwards we sometimes agonize about whether we made the right choice!) If the conflict is due to the existence of opposing ideas, attitudes, or pieces of information, the action may involve strengthening or altering the information to make it "fit." Thus if a person has two very good friends who intensely dislike each other, he can rectify the situation by changing his feeling toward one friend or improving the friends' relationship with each other. Sometimes conflicts are resolved by distorting or ignoring incoming information. If a TV commentator says something we do not want to hear, we may misinterpret the remarks or even turn off the set.

In selecting a course of action a manager can use knowledge about conflict as well as knowledge about frustration and anxiety. It is possible to diagnose a conflict situation by noticing the behavior exhibited. Too, it is possible to reduce conflict in a number of ways. We may supply information that supports a decision or belief. We may find means to work on two incompatible goals in sequence, so that eventually both may be achieved. A common source of conflict for employees is the variety of demands made on them by different parts of the organization. A secretary may have to answer the telephone whenever it rings but must also finish typing a report before a deadline. A foreman may tell a production-line worker to do a job one way but the time-study man may suggest another way. Classical management theories say these conflicts should not happen, but of course they do. Part of the manager's job is to recognize sources of conflict and help employees develop methods of dealing with them.

In each case, stress pushes us to react. We then behave in ways which (we hope) will relieve or reduce the discomfort we feel. Stresses, then, must be minimized in order to fulfill that basic need we discussed earlier: to avoid discomfort.

SUMMARY

Punishment and discipline are widely used to control behavior, but evidence indicates that these methods do not work as well as might be thought. Punishment may cause behavior to be hidden or suppressed in the presence of the punisher. A person will only abandon an undesirable behavior when performing it ceases to be rewarding. Thus punishment is not really the opposite or mirror image of reward. Punishment suppresses behavior rather than eliminating it from the list of potential behaviors.

Stress, like punishment, is uncomfortable. It occurs when goal-directed behavior is blocked (frustration), when there is uncertainty about the future (anxiety), or when a person must choose between alternative behaviors, goals, or information (conflict). These stresses act as "pushes" for behavior which reduces the stress. The manager's awareness of this

can help him or her diagnose and solve problems related to
on-the-job behavior.

SKILL DEVELOPERS

1. We try to infer, or figure out, what's going on inside a
   person from the behavior we see coming out. Think about
   the signs or behaviors which indicate that a person is experiencing stress. Can you think of someone who acts as
   though he or she is frustrated? Anxious? Experiencing
   conflict?
2. Describe the discipline system where you work, and compare it with another discipline system such as that in a
   school or university or a branch of the military.
3. Find someone who has recently made a very important
   decision, such as buying a house or car, or accepting (or
   rejecting) a job offer. Talk to the person about the decision and try to notice how the individual is handling
   any conflict about whether the right decision was made.

REFERENCES

NORD, WALTER R. "Beyond the Teaching Machine: The Neglected
Area of Operant Conditioning in the Theory and Practice of Management." *Organizational Behavior and Human Performance* 4
(1969):375–401.

PANEL DISCUSSION

In this section, the panelists discuss the need for discipline in organizations and their individual ways of applying discipline and upholding organizational rules and policies. They also consider handling their own negative feelings.

Lynne: I find it so much easier to go along and just accept the good behavior of the productive individual, and ignore them. But let someone else step out of line and immediately I know what I have to do.

Bob: One's negative and one's positive.

Lynne: I know it, but it's so much easier to be concerned with the negative. It's conspicuous. If I ignore the negative behavior, I won't have a functioning department for very long.

Phil: That employee's looking for some strokes, too.

Lynne: If I could get myself to the point of being regular about the positive, then I wouldn't have to put out so many negatives.

Bob: Probably. But regular does not necessarily mean repetitive, or the same. There should be a lot of variety and spice.

Jerry: When you develop as a manager, Lynne, then you achieve that goal. When you develop to your satisfaction, you'll be doing it automatically without even thinking about it. It comes naturally.

Lynne: All right—when you first learned, Jerry, were you consciously aware that this was what you were doing?

Jerry: Oh, yeah, sure.

Lynne: You set a goal for yourself each day.

Jerry: I always walk out on the floor and say, "Hey, you look sexy," or, "You look great." Or something like that just to stimulate them, and I use a different approach every time. It makes them feel better. I usually say something because I see something that turns me on.

Lynne: Bob, how do you feel about the positive strokes? What do you think about it?

Bob: I try to consciously do it. I try to let the person know that I've stroked—that I've taken time out of normal things to do it.

Lynne: But you still have to make an effort to do it.

Jerry: I don't always walk out on the floor every day, but when I do walk out on the floor it's automatic. I want to say something nice to somebody, and I want to dig somebody because I saw them do something wrong a day or two prior. When I walk out on the floor I always manage to walk through the plant. Not every day and not at every shift. I may go in on a Sunday, or on a Tuesday and I'll catch the first shift; but if I'm on the floor, it's automatic that I'm going to say something.

Bob: His presence demands that he do that. If he walks through and says nothing . . .

Jerry: You see the reason I say it's automatic—Bob hit on it. If I walk out on the floor and don't say anything—"What's he looking for; there's a problem?" Now if I'm loose—"How you doing; how was your day?" they know I'm just walking through, so it's a relaxed atmosphere. Because they can "smell" you.

Phil: Another aspect to that when you walk out there and you give these strokes, I think the stroke has got to be—it's got to be a specific kind of recognition.

Bob: To have any meaning.

Phil: Because if I walk up and say, "Hey, you're doing a fantastic job," you're going to say, "More bull."

Bob: I can see Jerry walking through the floor and saying, "I'm down here because I enjoy being down here and I like being with you people and walking through" and they're all relaxed.

Phil: It depends on the level of management. When Jerry walks out, you know, I get scared unless I know why.

Jerry: So what I do is I immediately break the ice. So it's a relaxed atmosphere.

Sue: I think what you said about being specific in referring to behavior is really important, and I was thinking of an example of that. I taught prekindergarten one summer at a ghetto school that was left open for the summer. There were about ten volunteers there who worked with the kids for the summer, and at the end of the summer the Mayor came to see the school with his entourage. They walked through and stopped at a girl, and the Mayor patted this girl on the shoulder and said, "Hey, you're doing a great job" and walked off. She said, "You know, all my life I've admired that man but I realized he had no idea whether I was doing a great job or not, and it didn't make me feel good. It made me feel bad, because I was getting this praise and he had no idea whether I deserved it or not."

Bob: He was giving something he couldn't give.

Jerry: Now, another thing I use is I give my negative strokes with humor. You know the knife—

Lynne: How do you know they're understood if . . .

Jerry: Oh, they're understood. I'll give you a specific example. I make it very obvious.

Lynne: Then why candy coat it?

Jerry: Because it gets to them and they feel that I'm not really mad, I'm annoyed. In other words, they measure it down the scale from one to ten. Give you a case in point. I've got a phobia about wasting pies. We have a lot of "cripples"; the machine chops a pie in half or a pie is busted. So they throw it into the garbage. Now there's no reason for that pie to go in the garbage. I have to pay to haul it away. We have the Thrift Store. When a pie is busted we have a little box where the girl is supposed to put the product. Then we have a girl in the Thrift Store who puts 10 or 15 pies in a bag, and we sell it as cripples. So we get two or three cents apiece for them, and the pie regularly sells for 25¢. So it's a good deal for the low-income people, and we do a tremendous business with people who come by to buy stuff for their freezers. So I go by and I say, "Gracie's brother-in-law is the hog man. He's picking up for the hog feed and she's making sure that his hogs are being fed. Gracie, why do you want me to pay for this stuff to be hauled away when we can sell the product?" and I smile. She knows what I mean. This is what I mean with humor.

Phil: Because you know your people.

Jerry: You've got to know your people or you can't pull it all the time.

Sue: I suspect that you use humor so people don't take you more seriously than you want them to take it. In other words, you don't want her to bust out crying. You just want her to think about it.

Jerry: Right.

Phil: I think that can really be effective. You've got to know how to use it. I've tried to use humor inappropriately, and when it boomerangs you get one of your pies in your face. I'll tell you, that's an unpleasant experience.

Jerry: That's the key thing for managers coming up. They've got to know their people. They can't manage out of a book. You've got to know the people.

Lynne: How do the rest of you handle negative comments?

Bob: You mean give negatives? Well, it depends on the person and what the subject matter is and how important it is. What Jerry's showing is awareness of a problem. That's all he's shown—that he cares about it and he's aware of it. That's kind of maintenance work really. But if it was really a specific problem then generally I like to isolate it, and call him in and do it sincerely.

Jerry: You don't read anybody down to a big audience, but on a one-to-one basis.

Bob: And before they leave you make sure they're O.K. "Did you hear what I said?"

Jerry: You don't chew anybody down.

Bob: "How are you taking it? Can we do something about it?"

Phil: It's personal. It's private.

Jerry: Right. You don't humiliate anybody.

Phil: Most managers, I think, have a tendency to do this: They pick a specific incident. Maybe Susie's screwed up— and then they say, "You're always doing this." You're afraid to really say, "God damn it, yesterday when you threw that pie away you pissed me off." Most people can deal with that okay. "Oh! I threw the pie away." But then the next thing is, "In fact, you're always costing us money." That's hard to prove. The thing Bob does is to check for understanding. "Are we together on this? Got that one?"

Bob: "And I'm not talking about firing you. I hope you didn't hear that. But I do want you to know that I'm damn unhappy about those pies, and I don't want it to continue."

Phil: Now people can respond to that. They can even deal with anger. If you're angry, you're angry.

Jerry: If you've got a basis for anger and they know that they're wrong they say, "O.K., you got me."

Bob: Anger is an honest emotion.

Phil: But it's the surface tension. "Hi, come on in; I want to talk to you about something" and the manager says, "How do you think you're doing on your job?"

Bob: "Oh, oh! Where are we going on this one?"

Phil: That's not important to the employee. What he's worried about is, "Do you think I'm good on my job?"

Sue: Lynne, I've tried to avoid making specific comments about women being different. I had a professor in business school that kept saying, "What's the women's point of view on this?" when I didn't think it differed from men's. But they just said anger is an important, honest emotion, and every manager ought to feel free to show anger. I'm not sure women have that same freedom.

Lynne: I think that it's much harder for a woman to actually allow herself to become angry. If I become angry I'm apt to cry, and I'd just as soon not do that.

Phil: It isn't ladylike to be angry, you know.

Lynne: Oh! I don't know about that.

Phil: But that's what a lot of women feel—they're boxed into that male vision of what it is to be a lady. If a lady is aggressive, or if she cries, then she ain't a lady anymore. Just like you said, the smart girls don't get the boyfriends. The compliant girls get the boyfriends.

Sue: I was wondering whether employees saw anger as being more "emotional" from a woman supervisor than they might ascribe to one of these guys. "He's angry because we didn't get the production out." Where they're tempted to say, "She's angry because she's an emotional person."

Lynne: I think that that's certainly apt to happen. I think women strive to be more objective and control their emotions, and try to have just the right setting. Probably not as much joking around—they're not as loose as men can be.

Bob: Well, we're not talking about uncontrolled anger, though.

Bill: Do you see your behavior as any different on the job than it would be if you were not in a supervisory position and you were someplace outside? Your feeling about anger and crying—do you feel you're in a special mode because you are a supervisor, and a woman supervisor, that you have to be different?

Lynne: No. I think I'm in a special mode because I'm me. Because again I don't want to fail. I don't want to look like a fool. I'm not going to blow my stack here, at work, or in a supermarket. If I want to blow my stack, I'll go home and close the door.

Sue: Like Jerry's tennis balls.

Jerry: That's just an outlet.

Phil: I think it's constructive and sometimes healthy to say that you're angry though, because they know it.

Lynne: You can admit anger without blowing your stack. "I'm very dissatisfied."

Bob: "I waited until today to talk to you because yesterday I was so mad I couldn't do it well. And I can do it well today, but I want you to know I was that mad."

Lynne: But that's objective.

Bob: You get their attention.

Lynne: You have it all together when you actually confront them with it. And if it takes you too long to get yourself together, then it's too late to do anything about their behavior.

Phil: Or maybe it really wasn't that important.

Sue: Do you think it's better when a manager or a supervisor sets up a specific discipline system? "Here's what's going to happen if the following things occur," or is it better not to have one, if you have your choice?

Phil: I think you'd better spell out whatever system you have. If there's immediate unpleasant consequences for breaking or violating certain regulations, people better know it.

Lynne: There are exceptions to the rule, too.

Bob: I would say that spelling out things are kind of like day-old threats and people don't operate the best under fear. So I would avoid saying, "Do it again, I'm going to fire you tomorrow." I'm going to say, "If it happens too often, you're going to force me into some kind of action." But don't spell out what that action is or when you'll measure it or any of that kind of thing.

Phil: There comes a time when you have to do that, though. There are people that just don't respond when you try to work with them. It seems to me sooner or later you talk about house rules and regulations. What happens if you steal things? Well, you get your ass fired. What happens if you're drunk on duty or smoke pot? You have to have some of those things written down someplace. Maybe it's in the employee manual or something like that. But it seems to me people ought to be apprised of the consequences of misbehavior on the job, one way or the other.

Jerry: Or breaking certain rules—"If you do this you're dismissed." In fact a couple of weeks ago I had to do something as stringent as that. They were messing with the formula and I put out a bulletin. "There are only two people in this organization who can change formulas. That's me and my quality control man, and if anybody's caught changing formulas he is immediately dismissed. Period."

Bob: How would they do that?

Jerry: Well, they thought they were doing me a favor. It was a small deal for a small particular customer, and it was inconvenient.

Bob: They wouldn't change the run.

Jerry: They wouldn't change the run. They thought they were doing me a favor, but they were really doing it for themselves, and so I just very simply said, "Look, the man is paying for a Cadillac with five wheels on it and you gave him a Cadillac with four tires. How would you feel if you paid top price? Would you like to be cheated? The man's paying the extra bucks for the product; he's entitled to what we said we're going to give him. I will not tolerate it. I'm not going to have anybody jeopardize the reputation that's taken me so many years to build." It was that simple.

Lynne: We're in the process of developing a blanket absentee control program. I really question it, we're coming out with a policy on tardiness. The second time you're tardy you'll have counseling; the third time you'll have a letter of warning —this sort of thing, and it covers tardiness, sick leave, unexcused absence, all of these things. I wonder how it's going to go over. Will it be a license for those people who don't abuse any of their privileges now?

Bob: What do they say? The last thing a dying company does is to rewrite all their policies?

Sue: I was thinking about a friend of mine who worked for an organization where the clients were mostly working people. So they put in many hours in the evenings and the weekends because you can't go in and interview somebody on an assembly line. You have to get them when they're free. So they got a directive about not coming to work tardy, and they just stopped seeing people on evenings and weekends. That's how they were compensating themselves for the extra work; they weren't putting in overtime, they were adjusting their hours. And it lasted a whole two weeks, I think. Then the directive had to be rescinded, because they couldn't complete any of their cases if they only saw the people they could see between eight and five.

Lynne: Well, I can see some problems with this policy that is being developed. I may have an individual who is abusing the rules about coming to work on time, but there may be someone else who has a flat tire one day and then maybe they're hit on the freeway the next week. It doesn't allow me any latitude to make that exception. The other employees are going to say, "She was late X number of times in a row and you didn't do a darn thing about it."

Bob: If your problems are with one or two people, deal with those. Don't make a policy for everybody else.

Lynne: It's out of my control.

Phil: You could use it as a guideline but not as a directive.

Lynne: We're saying the employees need to know what we expect of them. I expect them to be on time all the time.

Phil: To me that removes the supervisor from responsibility for regulating or scheduling the hours of work. What are you going to do about a guy who is always 10 minutes late but is a super, super performer?

Lynne: Depends on what his job is. If I need him there at 9:00, he better be there at 9:00.

Phil: But some jobs, people may not need to be there.

Bill: That kind of policy is just automating the supervisor's job. We talked about enriching jobs, and those kinds of policies can go all the way toward de-enriching the first-line manager's job.

Phil: Impoverishing the job, rather than enriching.

five

Self-Starting Behavior

OBJECTIVES

When you have completed this chapter, you should be able to:

1. Name some of the basic drives which produce self-starting behavior.
2. Explain creativity and innovation, and why they are needed in organizations.
3. Describe how participation works and how it reduces resistance to change.

BASIC SELF-STARTING DRIVES

In this chapter, we will examine various human behaviors to demonstrate that people are motivated by needs inside themselves and therefore act even when no outside forces are present. In other words these are behaviors people might show "on their own" without outside influence.

Psychologists consider *activity* a basic drive. It may be thought of as restlessness or the need to exert energy. In the past activity was thought to be linked to other needs such as hunger or thirst, since activity increases when these needs are present. However, both animals and humans desire activity even when no other basic drives are operating. We do not like to spend long periods of time motionless or even limited in our movements. This is important to realize when comparing Theory X and Theory Y, as in earlier chapters. If people were truly passive and lazy (as Theory X presumes), would the activity drive be so universally present?

There are other basic drives which relate to this question as well; for example, the *curiosity* drive, which also is found in both animals and humans. This urge to investigate may be expressed in ways such as sensory perception or through asking questions. It is related to other very similar drives, the exploratory drive and the manipulative (handling or using) drive. All are drives which motivate behavior even in the absence of physical needs or external rewards. In fact, people experimentally deprived of the opportunity to explore and manipulate become bored very quickly and then disoriented.

These drives also demonstrate the self-starting (or Theory Y) nature of motivation. It seems that we are not content just to experience what *comes* to us, but we *seek* new experiences as well. Self-starting behavior will occur when this need is felt. Thus we can expect people to be most satisfied when they can express their innate interest and curiosity.

Creativity

Another kind of self-starting behavior involves what we call *creativity*, associated most often with what we call the arts. Creativity is a difficult concept to define, although most of us feel we know it when we see it. It concerns the combining of ideas or concepts in new ways, resulting in new and innovative associations or discoveries. Thus an artist is creative if, using paints and a subject matter which have been used before, he or she combines these ingredients so that we think of or notice something we did not see previously.

Many jobs require creativity at some time. However, until recently many people believed that creativity was not a particularly useful resource for business organizations. It was assumed that organizations performed best when individuals' behavior was standardized, particularly in lower level jobs such as production or clerical work. Now more organizations are recognizing that creative abilities may be important in many areas, including those beyond the expected ones such as scientific research or advertising. There are times when every person in an organization must be creative, because formal rules and routines just cannot cover every situation that will arise. For example if a fire breaks out, the organization wants the employee to be creative fast, and DO something. Creativity must come from inside the employee; it cannot be the requirement of a policy manual or forced through orders. In fact employee groups or unions at odds with management sometimes find that doing everything "by the book," without using any of the creative solutions to routine problems which they have informally developed, is a good way to bring an organization to a standstill! These considerations have brought about more interest in learning how to identify creative people and in teaching people to be more creative.

One method of locating creative people is testing. Creativity tests generally ask a person to use ideas in a new way. One example would be, "Name as many uses of a brick as you can." Creative people are able to think of many uses, some of which are totally unrelated to a brick's most common use as a building material. Other tests evaluate a person's ability to create interesting word associations or to use a variety of geometric shapes in making pictures. The tests identify people who already have creative abilities and discover the people who can associate things with each other or provide a variety of new answers to old problems.

As we have said, interest is also growing in teaching people to be more creative. One popular method of improving creativity is *brainstorming*. Brainstorming works on the assumption that evaluating ideas too quickly prevents the development of better ideas. This technique tries to "hold off" the evaluation of ideas until many ideas have been generated. Thus in the discussion of a business problem, time is set aside for developing possible new solutions, thus eliminating comments such as, "We've already tried that" or, "It would cost too much" or, "It would never work." As a result, one idea will plant the seeds for other related and possibly better ideas. When many ideas are generated, the evaluation process can begin.

The idea of innovation is closely related to creativity. In order to be efficient and productive, most organizations must be aware of, and willing to adopt, new ways of doing things. They must also have individuals who can recognize situations where change is needed. Often organizations miss important opportunities either because employees hesitate to suggest new ideas or because changes are resisted by them. In order to deal with problems concerning employees, we must return to the idea of *participation* described in Chapter Two.

Participation

In discussing influence, we considered two ways in which organizations might use participative decision making, called the *human relations* and *human resources* approaches by Raymond Miles. The human relations model assumes that participation in organizational problem solving is desirable for the fulfillment of social needs. Employees are permitted to participate in minor decisions to make them feel a part of the organization. This may be a manipulative form of influence, if it is used by managers who believe that such participation really will not help the organization. These managers usually permit participation in decisions which have little importance, such as what color the lunchroom should be painted or whether there should be a company picnic. Managers also can restrict the employees' role in decision making, giving them predetermined alternatives to discuss and reserving the final decision for themselves.

On the other hand, managers who adopt the human resources approach encourage participation because they believe that the information and ideas generated by employees will help the organization. They feel that experienced workers will know how the work can be done more efficiently. In fact, most of us as *employees* feel this way ourselves. We say, "Why didn't they consult me before they designed this form?" or, "I could have told them this machine would continually break down." Thus the human resources approach considers productivity, not morale. Of course, if a person makes a suggestion which the organization really values and uses, it is likely to help fill the individual's esteem need. It gives the individual information about his worth to the organization and about his competence. We could predict that increased satisfaction of employees would result from using this approach.

Another benefit of participation is reduced resistance to change. Remember from Chapter Four that reactions to stress are particularly strong when the stress threatens need satisfaction (fulfillment) or self-image. We also stated that the prospect of change in a job or an organization can produce undesirably high levels of anxiety, because employees feel uncertain about the future. Moreover, it seems that simply providing a lot of information about the effects of a change is not enough to reduce the anxiety significantly. Thus attempts to eliminate resistance to change through communication alone do not seem to be successful. However, members of the group that has designed a change feel much less threatened by the change. These employees are able to follow the development of the change first hand and see that their individual interests are considered. They can also foresee much more accurately what the actual effects of the change are going to be. Therefore the threat of the new situation and the resulting anxiety are reduced, because there is less uncertainty about the future. As a result employees are more likely to cooperate and try to make the change work. They have less reason to ignore the change or sabotage it.

Participation is not a technique which is limited to formal use in large organizations. Anyone can use it at any time. In fact, in many small businesses it operates informally every day. The "boss" says to a worker, "Think of a way to handle those orders faster, will you?" The small business owner may ask employees for advice on which cash register to buy. Such people need advice and believe their employees have worthwhile opinions. Unfortunately in larger organizations this informal participation gets lost. The foreman or supervisor may feel that he or she would be showing ignorance by asking for opinions, or that seeking advice would look strange to higher level supervisors. Nonsupervisory workers are not the only people who resist change. Supervisors, managers, and even top-level executives may fear the possibility of confusion or loss of control if they encourage ideas and criticisms from their employees. However, the supervisor who is willing to overcome these apprehensions may find that he or she has tapped an important source of ideas for innovation and change which could improve the organization's overall performance.

A final example of what we have called *self-starting* behavior is Maslow's concept of self-actualization: the need to become a more mature, more complete human being. In Chapter One we stated that few people reach a point in their lives at which self-actualization motivates most of their behavior. However, all of us behave in this manner at some times. Behaviors motivated by self-actualization needs cover a wide range including those concerned with creativity. People paint pictures, write stories or poems, build furniture, or grow roses because they can express themselves through such activities. Other behaviors which fulfill self-actualization needs are those involved with helping others. Volunteering one's time to help old, sick, or disadvantaged people satisfies the need to express real concern for others. Yet another type of self-actualization behaviors are those through which people come to know themselves. Participation in religious activities, meditation, and psychotherapy are all ways people try to increase their self-awareness. As people mature, or progress up the need hierarchy, they will probably spend more and more time exhibiting self-actualizing behavior.

Some people are fortunate to have vocations which directly provide self-actualization. People involved in the arts or in scientific research may consider their occupations as "jobs" as well as their means of self-expression. Doctors, ministers, and teachers help people in their work. Such jobs are high in "intrinsic" satisfactions as discussed in Chapter Three. Many other occupations, however, do not provide opportunities for self-actualization. Thus people must seek fulfillment of this need outside of the work setting. One of the challenges, then, for successful managers is to discover ways to fulfill employees' higher-order needs on the job.

SUMMARY

In this chapter we have examined self-starting behaviors which are motivated not by outside influences, but rather by needs inside each person. Among them are the activity drive, curiosity, needs related to creativity, innovation, and change, and self-actualization needs which help us understand and express ourselves. Self-starting behaviors fulfill our needs through activities which are voluntary in nature.

Organizations benefit from members who exhibit self-starting behaviors, and it is important for the successful manager to learn to help employees develop them.

SKILL DEVELOPERS

1. What activities do you participate in for *yourself*, and not for pay or to fulfill obligations? Are there others in which you would participate if you had more time, or more money?
2. Is it a good idea to help a child develop personal interests such as musical appreciation, individual sports, hobbies or collections? If so, how can this be done? How do you feel about sports such as football which are less often pursued in adult life?
3. Think of two or three people you know well. What activities give them the most personal pleasure? Try to find out if you are correct.

REFERENCES

KOBAYASHI, SHIGERU. "The Creative Organization—A Japanese Experiment." *Personnel*, November–December 1970.

PANEL DISCUSSION

Here the panelists consider self-starting behaviors in themselves and their employees. They consider the need for creativity in organizations and the relation of social concerns
with respect to organizational success.

Sue: What differences do you see between work behavior
and the things you do voluntarily?

Bob: One thing that turns me on is when you get a well-
motivated person that signs on and they will come in on
Monday morning. They'll say, "I was thinking over the
weekend . . ." Almost everything exudes purpose, the
company purpose, you know, whatever their bag is. You'll
see him at a social gathering where there's five neighbors
and two of your people and all of a sudden your people
are talking.

Sue: O.K., but let's pull that around. What kinds of things
do you work at because *you* want to? That are voluntary,
whether they're charities or going fishing or . . .

Phil: You mean off the job?

Sue: Yes, and why do you do them?

Phil: O.K., why do we do what we do away from the job?

Sue: Do you see yourself as being pushed by your job? I
don't mean pushed in the bad sense of the word.

Jerry: To advance your job by doing certain things outside
the job?

Sue: Or complementing, for instance in the example I gave
of doing an activity in order to get something your job
doesn't give.

Bob: To develop a personality, to make me a whole person?

Phil: Who was it, Peter Drucker, that says that the successful businessman does something off the job that doesn't relate at all to his business, but really makes him a fulfilled individual. Maybe it's blowing clarinets, jazz band or barbershop quartets or collecting coins—something where he can feel accomplishment for what he does. Painting, for example, is a great out for people.

Bob: Sometimes you feel as though you just want a private thing that is just yours, that the company doesn't own.

Lynne: I found something for myself, that's all mine. And about six months ago I went into meditation. I took some instruction. I wouldn't give that up for anything. Twice a day the whole world is mine and I can do with it whatever I want.

Phil: I have something a little bit like that. I do a lot of running, and I run all by myself and I get as far away from other people as I can. I just think about things that I don't have a chance to think about otherwise and it's a very refreshing kind of thing, because you're out there gasping for breath and something happens.

Bob: I run every morning too, but I take 4 neighborhood dogs!

Phil: But I think it's important to have something that you do besides the job that fulfills you. Although there's nothing, I think, more fulfilling than doing a job well and coming home feeling, "I really did something great." And I don't think there's anything wrong with just being slothful from time to time—doing not a damn thing.

Lynne: You have to slow down and get rid of some of the stress.

Phil: I've never had the kind of responsibilities you have, but I suspect that if you have a good quarter and everybody pulls together and you make that bogey, it might be a great moment. It's like a peak experience because you've developed a cohesive team; they've achieved something together that they wouldn't have had you not been able to do that. At least that's what I would tell myself.

Bob: You also want to tell them that.

Jerry: You know, I know I personally got a lot of satisfaction when I built this new plant. I designed it in such a way that the executive offices are set up on a balcony. I've got a big picture window looking out on the plant. Every time I look out on that plant, I'll tell you, a feeling goes through me that's unbelievable. I finally knew what a woman feels like to have a baby. That's my baby. I don't care even if it's owned by Del Monte, it's mine. Because it's my invention; it's my creativity. There's not another business like it in the world. I invented the machinery and those people are working there because of me. Because I created it. Money can't buy it. You can't pay me for it. It's a great feeling.

What I do for creativity—I paint, but I miss the physical work, lifting the hundred pound sack of flour or stuff, so I play tennis. I got a ball machine and if I have a bad day I beat the hell out of those balls. I kill them and if I want to relax I just hit that ball machine for an hour, perfecting my strokes. I serve 'til my arm falls off. So I get that relaxation. Sometimes I do it to let off steam.

Phil: Hard physical activity. I like to do that too.

Jerry: You need it, you know. You can't afford to beat your wife, because of the laws.

Phil: Plus they sometimes hit back.

Jerry: I get involved with charities, as anonymously as I possibly can, because I can't stand the guy who wants his name in the paper. I was brought up, for the lack of a better term, on the other side of the tracks. We were very poor people. I feel very lucky that I was able to make it. It's not that I'm so bright, because I think there's a lot of brighter guys around. There are guys I went to school with who are still working and not making big bread, and I feel very humble about it. So I'm a soft touch.

Phil: Well, it may be, too, coming from the environment that you came from you didn't have a hell of a lot. It really served as a goad to work that much harder.

Jerry: There's not much doubt about it. It was my own motivation. My kids are not motivated at all. They don't know what it is to live without a swimming pool. They don't know what it's like not to have their own bathrooms. I slept on the couch. I slept in attics.

Phil: You kind of slept around. . . .

Bill: This question on environment in terms of its effect on motivation, I think is a very important one. Sue and I have a colleague in academia who tells the story in the area of motivation about the problem that they were having at Yellowstone Park with the bears. They kept raiding the camps and the garbage and everything else. Well, you have to motivate those bears to change their behavior because that's what you do in motivation. Now you can't go down there and sit down with the bears and say, "Now let us reason together." You've got to change the environment and so what do you do? You put on cans that have locks and tight lids on them that the bear can't get to and things like that. You change the environment, and that's the way you motivate the bears to change their behavior. Well our environments, I think, do create a lot of the motivation for us to behave in a certain way. Your environment and mine, Jerry—I came from the same background—probably gave us some of the same motivations.

Jerry: But I'll tell you something that's interesting, I was just thinking about. When I sold out in 1968, my son had just graduated from high school and was going to college. He thought I was a slave driver. I should really share all this with my employees. There was no doubt about it. I was an abuser of the working class. I said, "I don't see you sleeping out there in the garage." Now time has passed. He's down at the University of California for his Ph.D. and you'd be surprised. This kid has turned into a hell of a conservative. It's amazing how he flip-flopped. He's gotten to be way, way over to the other side because he says, "Hey, *we* should manage." I mean, there's no middle of the road. Hopefully he'll come back. Now he's very conservative. Those who got it know how to manage better than the working people and the uneducated. We can do a better job. I say, "Hey, baby, you know about the caste system?" But he's beginning to change a little bit again, but I guess it's a cyclical thing kids go through. I've always said it's normal for a kid at the age of 20 or 21 to be communistic oriented in our society because the inequities are so vast—the haves and the have-nots.

Phil: They are much more easily perceived.

Jerry: So I don't think that's anything unhealthy. It's unhealthy when they get to be around 30 and they are still thinking that way.

Lynne: But we all go through life trying on different ideas. Trying them on to see if they fit, if they're comfortable. Maybe you choose to wear them.

Jerry: Well, they don't just try them on but they really believe it. That's the sad part. He really believed at that time that I took advantage of the workers.

Lynne: I really believed things too, yesterday, but today I don't necessarily feel the same.

Bill: When you try them on you *should* believe them.

Bob: Do you think he believed so much that if you'd given him that money and said, "Now, if you want to give it to those employees you can,"—that he believed it *that* much?

Jerry: I don't know.

Bob: Because that would be the real test.

Jerry: Well, now he has money of his own and I don't see him giving it away.

Phil: It's interesting about the leftist orientation of young people, and as they grow older and as they gain more experience, I think they suddenly realize that no one dogma is going to solve the problems of the world. In fact, the Italian Communist Party, which is in a position to almost take over the government, doesn't want it now.

Jerry: Of course not. "I don't want to be involved and *run* this country. We just sit back here and snipe."

Phil: "Hey, we can't do any better than the Social Democrats can!" The problems are so inter-related now that no one dogma can probably address them successfully.

Sue: Well, I guess that's something I'm interested in taking a look at. You commented about no one person can solve everything or no one person can change things. Do you see in the future more demands, or fewer demands, from employees that "this company ought to be more involved in charities" or "you ought to give me time off to be in the Peace Corps"?

Bob: Much more; one of the questions I'll be asked is, "What things does your company do to fulfill social responsibility? How many sabbaticals do you have in this company?"

Jerry: You have the thing with jury duty that they get their pay.

Bob: Profit sharing.

Jerry: I mean there's more social conscience in a large corporation, or any corporation, and I think it's a healthy thing.

Sue: Do you think employees are a part of the push to cause this?

Jerry: Right. The younger employees. Not the older ones. The younger employees, the young people coming on stream. They are, and hopefully they will get more, involved with politics.

Phil: Which raises an interesting question because there is a move, I think especially in this area—northern California seems to be very progressive in terms of those kinds of benefits. But, you know, as we give more vacation time and as we provide sabbaticals—as we, for example, increase jury duty time, personal time, personal leave and so forth, we encourage people to get more involved in community activities. Not one of those damn things can be enjoyed on the job. How do you motivate people in some cases? Well, we'll give you more time off. We'll give you a few more days of vacation. What I'm really concerned about is how you can get people to commit 100 percent of their energies to the work.

Bob: I don't think that would be healthy either.

Jerry: But 100 percent, that's too much.

Bob: Individuals at 100 percent are no longer individuals.

Jerry: No. They're machines.

Phil: But I sometimes think that we do harm by focusing too much on these off-time extracurricular activities.

six

Motivation of Groups and Organizations

OBJECTIVES

When you have completed this chapter, you should be able to:

1. Explain what a group is, and how it affects its members.
2. Describe some goals or objectives which are common to all groups and organizations (systems).
3. Explain how congruence (or lack of it) between group and organizational goals might affect performance.

GLOSSARY

Cohesive Sticking, holding, or clinging together.
Congruent Corresponding, agreeing, harmonious.

GROUPS AND ORGANIZATIONS

So far we have considered the motivational process in regard to single individuals. However, it is also important to consider the motivational factors involved when dealing with groups of people and organizations. It is tempting to think of a group as a human being, having similar feelings and reactions; but this will lead to some wrong assumptions and predictions. Chapter Six will deal with some of the special aspects of motivating organizational groups.

We may think of a *group* as a collection of people with a common goal or objective. The "motivation" of such a group seems clear—the common goal. However, we must take into account another important consideration. For example, all the people on a certain plane might have a common goal—to reach Los Angeles. However, they do not need to interact with each other to achieve that goal. A more precise definition of a group then would be a collection of *interdependent* individuals with a common objective. In other words, a group exists whenever related actions of its members are required to reach some predetermined goal.

The leader of a group has various responsibilities with respect to this goal. It may be necessary for the person to explain the goal itself, to channel the group's overall activities in directions to achieve the goal, or to channel individual behaviors to mutually satisfy the members and the group. The leader may use any or all of the methods of influence discussed earlier: authority, manipulation, collaboration, or even coercion.

Of course, influence within groups is reciprocal. The members influence each other and the leader just as the leader influences them. In some groups, the members may have individual or informal collective goals which differ from, or even contradict, the official objective of the group. This is particularly true of groups whose members join for instrumental reasons (for example, to earn money) rather than to support the group's goals. Assembly line workers, for example, may care very little about the company or the product. They may form informal groups in order to make the time pass more quickly or even to cause disruptions. Sometimes the members may try to convince their leader to ignore behaviors directed toward achieving informal goals of the group, rather than the official company goals. This may become a source of conflict for the leader or supervisor, as we discussed earlier. Different parts of the organization expect different behaviors from the supervisor.

We all have needs for affiliation, and therefore groups are important for everyone to some extent. However, groups fulfill other needs as well as the need for affiliation. They can provide support; that is, they can provide a setting in which to learn appropriate behavior in given situations. They can help to fulfill esteem needs by giving members feedback on performance or personal worth.

When a group succeeds in fulfilling its members' needs, the members will consider the group desirable and membership in it very valuable. This feeling generates a "stick-togetherness" we call *cohesiveness*. Cohesive groups are able to attract and keep members and to satisfy their goals. (Of course the goals may not be the same as those of the larger organization to which they belong.) A group can exert strong forces on its members, influencing them to behave in ways which help them maintain their membership. For that reason, members may dress or talk similar to others in the group or behave in ways which the group approves. The group has *norms* or standards of behavior required of members; if a person wants to be a member he must behave accordingly. Thus the group serves as a motivator, causing the individual members to act in certain ways.

Sometimes we think of this motivation as pressure to conform and hastily assume that the consequences are negative; but in fact, the consequences may be either desirable or undesirable. Groups may develop norms of high productivity or other standards which are beneficial to the individuals and the organization. The fact that most people belong to more than one group serves as a check on too much conformity. (A person who conforms totally to the norms of one group would not fit into any other.) We rely on conformity to a large extent when we manage people. We assume that people will react in predictable ways, or that they will not want to be "different."

The Hawthorne Studies

One famous project which discovered the motivational effects of groups was known as the "Hawthorne Studies."

This series of research projects, named after the manufacturing plant in which the research was done, began as a relatively simple project to determine the effects of physical factors, such as lighting and rest periods, on productivity. At one point the researchers separated a small group of women from the main manufacturing area and placed them in a smaller room. Within a short time, the researchers were puzzled to find that the changes they made experimentally increased the women's productivity, even when it was least expected (such as when the level of lighting was drastically *lowered*). The experimenters searched for a reason for this unusual result and finally concluded that it was change in the social setting of the group, not in the work methods, which caused increased productivity. The group members, and thus the group itself, were motivated to work harder because they found the changes pleasant and wanted them to continue. They enjoyed the smaller, more casual workroom, the ability to interact with each other, and the pleasant supervision of the researchers. They appreciated being asked for their opinions of the changes and their suggestions for future changes. The Hawthorne Studies thus brought out the importance of social and group factors in the behavior of employees.

In another part of this project a group of men were observed at their jobs over a long period of time. They were found to be exceptionally uniform in their productivity; each week's production was about the same, and the productivity of each member was very similar from week to week. The workers were practicing *work restriction;* that is, they held back and did not produce more than an informally agreed upon amount. They also saved up finished products from a good week to compensate for a less productive week. The group disapproved of members who either worked much less or much more than the average. In this case, group factors had provided the motivation to restrict, rather than increase, productivity. Members who wanted to remain part of the cohesive group obeyed its norm and were therefore less productive than they could have been.

The two examples from the Hawthorne Studies focus our attention on the subject of group goals and how they affect motivation. In a given situation we would expect to find that an organization has goals, and that it assigns to the existing groups goals which are the same as its own, or which will contribute to the attainment of its own goals. Yet we often find that the groups have developed goals of their own as well. Recall the women in the first part of the Hawthorne Studies. As a group they developed a goal which was compatible with, or congruent to, the goal of the larger organization. Thus the group members were motivated to work toward the organization's goal because doing so also helped them to attain their goal as a group. The men in the second example developed a goal that was incompatible with that of the larger organization; they feared that higher productivity might cause one of them to be laid off. In both examples the groups were cohesive and were able to impose certain norms on their members. The difference noted in their productivity resulted from the difference in compatibility of their goals with those of the larger organization. Thus cohesiveness was not the deciding factor.

Objectives of Organizations

We noted earlier that it is dangerous to assume that an organization always reacts like an individual. However, we also stated that systems theorists wish to discover factors which all systems have in common. Thus we can speak of organizations being motivated, much like individuals or groups. Systems theorists generally agree that all systems have objectives and that those objectives may be defined as the survival, growth, and satisfaction of all of its parts (or members). So we could expect to find that organizations are motivated by these same objectives.

In *The Planning Process*, there is a more detailed discussion of organizational objectives and goal setting. But even from our own observations we might conclude that organizations have goals in the survival, growth, and satisfaction categories. For example, they usually want to avoid losing money, which would generally cause failure to survive. They want to increase profits, gain more members, or have more branches—all signs of growth. And in order to achieve these objectives an organization must be able to attract and keep employees or members—in other words, to satisfy them.

Organizational Influence

An organization is simply a vehicle for working efficiently. It cannot act on its own and must have members or employees to act for it. So, it must be able to influence people to behave in certain ways. First, it must attract them to join the organization. Then the organization must influence them as members to behave reliably: to attend work, do their tasks, and follow the rules. (This would be true in a profit-making firm, a nonprofit organization, or even a voluntary club.) Finally, although we sometimes neglect this phase when thinking about organizations, the organization must influence members to act in innovative ways, at least some times. It just is not possible for an organization to create a rule for every situation; sometimes an employee must act independently, for example, in an emergency. Too, the organization wants employees to cooperate with each other in a variety of situations, although it may be impossible to describe all of them in a policy manual. This area of independent, creative behavior is so important to the running of real-life organizations that workers have used strict adherence to the rule book as a good way of slowing down or stopping organizations, as we noted in Chapter Five. Written rules cannot take everything into account.

In order to influence independent behavior, the organization does many things. It develops leaders, managers, or supervisors, who have direct responsibility for transmitting organizational goals to their subordinates, assigning specific tasks, and so forth. Of course there are many kinds of groups within organizations, and the amount of influence the leader has will vary. There are groups that have the same boss ("command groups"). There are groups that work together on the same task. Then there are "informal" groups that do not relate directly to the formal job design or chain of command. Their members may only share common interests or goals or enjoy each other's company socially. Since the memberships of these groups may overlap, it is not unusual for a work group to have a formal leader (a foreman or supervisor) and an informal leader (a well-liked member) as well.

Another way organizations elicit desired behavior is through communication. Members must have a way of knowing what the organization expects of them. Communication systems disseminate this and other types of information. Another book in this series, *Communicating in Organizations* by Rockey, discusses this important topic.

We have discussed another method used by organizations to influence behavior: creating systems of reward. In an organization whose members are employees, some rewards are the *hygiene factors* which help to reduce dissatisfaction and attract new employees, factors such as pay, health and retirement benefits, vacation policies, and the like. Some are the *motivators*, or intrinsically satisfying rewards, such as the importance of the job itself, status, the opportunities for recognition, advancement, or promotion, and so on.

Organizations which do not hire or pay their members may use slightly different reward systems. It is likely, for example, that a member of such an organization has joined because the individual had a direct interest in its goals. Since most people need to work to provide income a person joining a nonpaying organization usually cannot be involved in its activities full time. Therefore we can expect rewards to be a "mix" of those which are intrinsic to the job or organization and those which enhance the value or attractiveness of the work.

Organizations seem to work best (get the most commitment from their members) when the goals of the organization and the goals of the individuals working in it are the same, or at least compatible; their goals fit together so that the employee or member can attain personal objectives by doing things at the same time which contribute to organizational goals. Here lies another answer to the question, "How can I motivate employees?" Managers provide important inputs to the motivational process by (1) providing ways for employees to reach their goals while achieving the goals of the company and (2) by helping employees see how this can be done.

SUMMARY

Groups and organizations greatly influence the motivations of their members. When a person values membership in a group, the individual is very likely to behave in ways that the group approves. Strongly cohesive groups can produce either high or restricted productivity, depending on the group's concern for the organization's production goals. All organizations have goals and objectives, and they need members or employees to carry out these goals. In order to attract and keep members, organizations develop systems of leadership, communication, and rewards.

SKILL DEVELOPERS

1. Think of an organization which you belong to or know about. What are some of the formal or informal groups in it? Which people belong to more than one group?
2. Describe a group you have been part of whose goals are the same as or congruent to those of the larger organization. Then describe another group which has had goals in addition to or in opposition to those of the larger organization.
3. Name some ways in which groups to which you belong might get you, or another member, to "go along with" the group's wishes even if you did not want to.

REFERENCES

CARTWRIGHT, DORWIN, AND LIPPITT, RONALD. "Group Dynamics and the Individual." *International Journal of Group Psychotherapy* 60 (1957):86–102.

PANEL DISCUSSION

In this section the panelists discuss how they work with groups. They consider the advantages and disadvantages of creating task groups and also ways of motivating existing groups.

Jerry: One time the general manager was being "buffaloed" by the people in the plant because they knew he had no production background, so they had told him something couldn't be done. I said, "Well, look, I'll give you 36 hours. If they say they can't do it, I will personally come in and do it. But when I come in and do it there's going to be some heads chopped." In 18 hours that thing was cleaned. This was chocolate. It was very ugly. And they said, "We couldn't clean this because it had a lot of electric wires." I said, "Well, how did all the other companies do it? It doesn't make sense. And if we can't in fact clean it we throw it away and we knock off the line, because we're not jeopardizing a billion and a half dollar company selling salmonella." Well, they got the thing cleaned and basically what was it? The machine was placed about twenty feet from the floor drain and when you hosed it down you had to get a squeegee and bend down and squeegee it to the floor drain.

Bob: Unpleasant job.

Jerry: Right; and they didn't want to bend down; they didn't like it. Afterwards, they were so proud, and I said, "Great. I always want to see it like that." But people will push as far as they can to make their job easier; and it's also a game to see, "How well informed is this boss? Does he really know what's going on?" Test, they're always testing a new guy.

Sue: Well, I think particularly in routine jobs or in jobs that you've had for a long time, that is kind of a motivation; it's a way of keeping things interesting. There are some people who are very highly productive on production line jobs because they play games with themselves, and see if they can beat their level or do it a different way instead of the same thing; and I suspect that beating the dealer is another kind of a game. I've always felt the people like to have control over their own lives; and if they can't control anything but how many problems they can create, then that's what they're going to control.

Jerry: You know, there's another point that should be interesting with this book, especially with young people coming up. I know from personal experience that when you put somebody in a managerial level they can't help a feeling of superiority against the working class, because that working class will kill them and it'll ruin them, and they'll make their job untenable. I had an experience; I had to relieve a man who was on the job eight years. He had this father-son relationship and the production people got resentful, and would only do things on direct orders. If they knew the direct order was going to foul up the production line, they would do it purposely because they resented this relationship. And he always talked down to them. And you don't talk down to people; you've got to talk to them on their level. And this is very important, especially with young managers coming out—that they don't feel "I've got a college education; you're just dumb; just keep putting that stuff in the box." We recently had to give a credit—the girls were bagging empty bags of peanuts. We were selling to an airline and they wanted a refund and rightly so. The girl on the packing line knows you don't put an empty bag with no nuts into a box you sell for peanuts. But they hated the new manager. There's a new man on the street, and they didn't like him. "Well, we're going to fix his wagon."

Phil: You reap what you sow.

Jerry: How are you going to blame anybody, because you've got five girls on the line? But this is a problem with managers. Especially young managers who don't have the experience with the human resources.

Sue: Well, we've been talking primarily about individuals here; but you mentioned five girls on the line, and maybe we ought to talk a little bit about groups. Is there a concept you can use, group motivation, or do groups have goals or motivation?

Jerry: Yes, in our operation we have three shifts. You ride one shift about efficiency and a goal, if they can win a dinner or some sort of a challenge, and you keep a record on how much waste one group creates while the other doesn't. Those are basically old simplified things that we've used for years.

Bob: The trouble is when you get to committees. Committees don't get fired but people do; committees don't get promoted but a person does; and there is a real motivational problem and reward and penalty problem when you create committees that have a specific task. This is the finance committee or this is the new sales committee or something like that. Because how do you motivate that group when there's nothing in it for any individual one of them? Either in reward or punishment. I'm beginning to think that the only way out of that is to give that responsibility to one person. And say to them, "I hope you form a committee to advise you. But that job, that responsibility, that goal is yours."

Lynne: Do they say that teams don't pay off?

Bob: Yes, teams do pay off. They pay off tremendously when you get that collection of background material, new ideas, they synergize themselves. But how do you reward, how do you motivate that group as a group?

Lynne: But do you really make any more money having teams than you do having individuals? I'm curious. We've run MBO and task force and all this, and I really question whether it has improved our efficiency at all.

Bob: I think there are times when you get a broader spectrum of inputs. Plus you get exchange of knowledge, exchange of communication, good personal relationships.

Lynne: Dollars and cents, is it better?

Jerry: One good thing about the committee is you get much better communication because everybody's there.

Lynne: So their needs are fulfilled.

Jerry: What I was going to say in reference to Bob is about the way you reward, if you're able to get a committee of self achievers. If you get up in the higher level, basically most of the people in the higher level are usually self-achievers. And if they're self-achievers, you have no problem. But when you don't have a self-achiever in there, then watch out.

Phil: If you structure the team so that you use your resources to the best advantage, if you get a guy that maybe isn't a self-starter, if that guy's got all the knowledge in the world about your project, I don't care if he isn't a self-starter as long as he's a communicator. And if you can structure your organization or your project team or your group as long as you've got representatives from different functions, so that you can get the job done or at least a good recommendation based on what they say; then you've got something. But I think Jerry's point about getting the people together is really important because so many times projects get delayed because Charlie's out of town and Chuck's got a meeting; you can spin your wheels.

Bob: They can also work against you because pretty soon

you say, "I wanted that done" and they say, "The committee decided not to."

Phil: "The project team said it was impossible."

Lynne: What do you do then?

Bob: Well, I don't have the answer; but I'm starting to think it's appointing one person responsible and saying, "If you want to form a committee, I think it's a good idea. But when that thing doesn't get done, I am going to you. You use the committee, fine; it's your choice. But you to me, I want it done."

Lynne: So you give the individual task, and he does it his own way.

Jerry: That's the only way to do it. You assign it.

Phil: Fixed responsibility.

Sue: Well, I guess I'm seeing a different kind of situation. I'm thinking about the case in which the interdependency exists already, rather than saying we're going to pull together a team for a special project. There are eight guys in this assembly situation or there are four people who answer these telephones. I think you've been talking more about the situation where the person is doing more of an information gathering function.

Bob: You're talking about a work team?

Sue: Yes, a work team, where they don't have any choice. You can't say one of you will bag peanuts; they're all in fact bagging peanuts. Does this make a difference in what you would say about groups and motivation?

Jerry: Well, if everybody's bagging peanuts you should get

them together and say, "Has anybody got a better idea on
how you bag or how I bag? Which one is more efficient?"

Bob: What's your biggest problem? Not as an individual; but
as a group, what is your biggest problem in making this job
better? Getting improved production results. I think we can
motivate them as a group.

Jerry: People still do have a sense of pride, and you've got
to get to it.

Phil: I think a lot of this is having a good infrastructure of
supervisors who lead people. In management, if you're talking about that level, if you're talking about the lower level
jobs the supervisor is typically the forgotten man in the organization. He's the guy who really is responsible for direct
person-to-person contact.

Jerry: The middle management is usually where the weakest
link is.

Bob: They're the ones who generally get promoted for the
wrong reasons.

Bill: That's why we're leaning toward the supervisory and
first level manager; they're the key people and that's why
we think this area is so important.

Phil: Most of the training and teaching I do is at the first
level; and these people are pretty pragmatic people—they
like the hands on, how do you do it? "I'm not interested in
the Maslow and the Herzberg; help me *do* it."

Bob: Do today's job better.

Jerry: Well, the way I get them to do it, and I've been successful with my middle management people, is I make them
start off at the lower level even though I'm paying at the

middle management level. I get them to do the menial job and my advice to them is very simply, if you know how to do it nobody can BS you. You've been there. You paid your dues. So you're getting the advantage of maybe not getting the low salary, but you're doing the job; and I only want you to do the job until you know it well so you can say, "Wait a minute, whoa, I've been there." And the lower echelon respects you for it.

Sue: I wish it worked the other way. Because you have the problem that the best research scientist isn't always the best manager, and the best salesman is not always the best sales manager and so forth. And certainly the best typist is infrequently the best office manager.

Bob: And the best bagger of peanuts is not always the best foreman.

Phil: On the other hand, the worst bagger may make a very good manager. If I screw up bad enough I might get promoted!

Jerry: And this is what management is all about, you know, really getting to know the people on a one-to-one basis. But they're not numbers.

Phil: To me the key to what you're talking about, especially in routine kinds of jobs where you've got four or five people performing basically the same duty is getting a supervisor who knows those people, because groups can form, they can combine to become a very cohesive force, and they can limit production. The Hawthorne Studies tend to prove that if nothing else. And let's face it, if you get a new guy on the line who ups production a little bit all of a sudden the group gets a little negative about that. But a supervisor who's been there and comes up through that rank can identify some of those problems and then you're going to be ahead of the game.

Jerry: And the people identify with him because they know that he was one of them, and they'll work for him.

Bob: They expect him to change once he's made a supervisor, but not too much. He's still got to think of them as he did when he was one of them.

Phil: That might suggest another area for you to address in that book. What kind of role do you follow as you've been promoted? How do you communicate? A lot of people feel an experience of uptightness about that because before they're all buddy-buddy and now they're the boss.

Bob: "Now he does nothing; he used to work."

Jerry: Well, I know with some of my management that when you promote them internally, when things get real rough they'll say, "Why don't you put me back in the unit; let me get back in the lower level."

Bob: What I've found, Jerry, is that when you have a work group and you want to promote a person to supervise that work group, frequently if you'll send him away for six months and then bring him back people will imagine that during that six months he learned skills. Then he comes back different. He isn't just promoted from one-day-there to next-day-boss. And so that period of absence is good.

Lynne: Do you have to send him away for training during that six-month period?

Bob: No, job rotation.

Jerry: See, you're fortunate you can do that because you have a situation where you can ship them to another part of the country.

Bob: You can put them on a different shift.

Jerry: We usually do those things. But usually we've found that if they've been promoted within that shift, the shift itself says, "Well, he's earned it" and they'll keep the same level up. Because he knows them, Bob, so you have acceptance prior to the post.

Jerry: If you don't have acceptance, then you have a problem, then you switch shifts. But usually we've found that they have acceptance. If the guy really performs better than the others they'll get on him. And if he backs down he's not managing material; but if he fights them and they finally accept him, you've got a strong manager.

Bob: Then that's how you make the choice.

Jerry: That's how I do make my choices in fact.

Lynne: How do you cope with the union then in that decision?

Jerry: Well, we have seniority and the way you do it is according to this contract, to post the job. And then there's seniority people—they have five days.

Lynne: How do you prove merit and ability is what I'm asking. You have two people. They've been working side by side for five years; both are doing acceptable jobs. One's doing a little better than the other and is the junior employee. You really want to promote that one, but you have a seniority factor with the other one who has been doing satisfactory work. Now how do you document, how do you convince the union that you should go ahead and promote the junior?

Jerry: Well, the way you do it is by posting the job and the senior puts in for the job and you say he can't do it.

Lynne: But what I'm asking you is what do you have to back you up?

Jerry: It's just a judgment decision you don't need anything to back up.

Bob: Some unions you do and some you don't.

Jerry: The prime thing is that they have got to have desire, being part of this thing. If the guy doesn't like the restaurant business he should get the hell out.

Sue: But if we're trying to help a young manager who's trying to go to work today, he can't always assume, the first day he walks onto the job, that everybody is turned on to the goals of Saga Foods, or whatever. It's kind of unfair to our readers to say, "Take it for granted that all your people are turned on when you get them and that they ought to respond to this." Can't we talk for a little bit about that?

Bob: We should start with the selection process.

Phil: It seems to me we start with the staffing area a little.

Bob: Well, I think matching their goals and identifying with goals. Start with the proper hiring and selection process and trying in the initial hiring better to say, "Our company's going in this direction, doing these things, and this life style, and this is realistic to expect. Now does that turn you on, or what are you expecting? Do you have a career path laid out for yourself individually? Do you know what your talents are? Do you know what price you're willing to pay?"

Sue: But when I walk on that job I'm most likely going to have employees that are already there. Jerry doesn't hire a supervisor and say, "O.K., you go out and hire 18 guys to run this shift." That supervisor inherits people and I don't think he can make this assumption necessarily.

Jerry: You kind of get to know them.

Bob: When you get to know them you say, "Why are you here? Why are you doing what you're doing? Tell me about yourself. I'll tell you about myself."

Phil: But one of the most important things a new manager can do or a new supervisor, or a new whatever, in his organization is to get to know his people on a one-to-one basis. And to really spell out to them his interpretation of the company goals.

Bob: "Here is my philosophy of management. Here's the way I'm going to conduct myself."

Phil: You take a look at the selection process. I think that's so important, reinforcing what Bob said because we don't often accent that. The military—the Marine Corps, for example. The fact that they stress, "Are you good enough to be in this organization? It's tough; we're going to make a man out of you. It's going to be a bitch." And people expect that when they go in they're committed pretty much from the start. O.K., if you can emulate or replicate that in an industrial organization—"Hey, it's going to be rugged; these are the demands."

Bob: IBM did it a few years ago. The striped ties and the blue suits.

Phil: And if you don't buy into it then you don't have to join us.

Lynne: But, Sue, aren't you talking about the manager who inherits a department and the employees are there from the clerks right on, and how you're going to motivate those people?

Bill: That's what you had, Lynne.

Jerry: I did the same thing—I just inherited a candy company.

Lynne: I think your own modeling, the modeling you do.

Jerry: That's exactly right.

Lynne: You can't appeal to everyone.

Jerry: But it was very simple. I walked in and I just said I didn't ask for the job. I was asked to take over. I'm here to help and you fellows know more about the candy business than I do because I never made candy, and you have. Our plant manager was making candy. He's 34 years old and has been making candy for 18 years. And I said I've never been a failure or a loser and it goes against my grain and I'm not looking for it. But I will admit that there has been a certain amount of fear of God.

Phil: They know why.

Jerry: They know I'm there and because of my physical size I intimidate people.

Phil: You're kind of mean looking at that, Jerry.

Jerry: I tell them right off the bat I mean I won't tolerate some things. It's been rough going and you have a heavy hand when you have to. Again that's the discretion of the manager.

Bill: Do you feel you are changing their expectations about what a manager was like as versus the previous manager?

Jerry: Yes, very definitely, because it was a definite different ideology again. They put a guy in charge who came out of a different environment. He came out of a large environment when he had qualified adjutants under him. He gave an order and they followed up. I don't think the guy ever walked into a plant. He was a typical executive vice president in a large corporation. The corporation made the mistake.

Phil: You sound like you're almost 180° from him. You seem like a hands on type. To know the basics, to know the fundamentals, to run the store. You pick the right people who know the fundamentals.

Sue: Well, then I see you going into a new department intimidating people with your physical size. Lynne, can you contrast the way you came into your situation with that?

Lynne: Being low key to start with, I made up my mind not to make drastic changes and recognizing the fact that there were professionals in the department, and leveling with the people that I like what I'm doing and I'm here to help you. I think being excited about the work myself. All of a sudden there was some camaraderie in the whole thing and there really was someone who cared.

Bill: The enthusiasm is contagious.

Bob: They expect that from a boss.

Jerry: And the boss, when things are rough, has to be positive and he's got to be hopeful.

Lynne: I think you also have to be very honest. That some days you really don't feel very good about the whole thing. "This is my day and I'm down."

Jerry: I walked into a situation in the candy company. Eighty-five percent of our raw material is sugar. O.K., sugar hit the plateau of $62.00. It went from 10¢ a pound to 60¢ a pound. So I said, "Look, there's no way we are going to make any money; but we are going to try. If we break even we're going to be damn lucky, but sugar's not going to stay at $60.00. Our day will come. One of these days the bill is going to go up and the market is going to drop. So we better be prepared when it drops down." Because we're making a penny ball of bubble gum and the kid doesn't have a nickel, and the machines can't take a nickel. So you've got to put out a penny ball of bubble gum, and you can't make the thing any smaller 'cause it won't fit the machines. So I said, "Any ideas that you may have we'll try. The corporation can handle the loss, so don't feel bad, because there's nothing we can do about it. But when the market drops, and it will, that's when we'll go. But in the interim let's try. We won't be able to do it overnight, but we're not expected to." Just build some confidence because they were losing money for so long. I told them, "I've got news for you; it's not going to be a way of life with me. If this thing can't survive I'll padlock the door and we'll place you elsewhere. We're not a nonprofit organization."

Phil: That positive orientation is contagious. I think another technique that a manager can use when he takes over an operation is not only in addition to the positive orientation or the enthusiasm and the modeling of good behavior, is to be willing to listen to people. I think one of the most important things a good manager can do is really listen and react and respond and give an honest answer. Maybe an employee has a great suggestion on how to do something. It may or may not be practical but at least have the opportunity to air that. To have some air time. It's really important. The best managers I've ever worked for may have bought maybe 25 or 30 percent of what I've suggested to them, but at least they listened to me and that fulfilled a pretty important need for me.

seven

Some Uses of
Motivational Ideas

OBJECTIVES

When you have completed this chapter, you should be able to:

1. Identify some specific uses of motivational concepts in business organizations.
2. Explain why these programs "work," in motivational terms.

USES OF MOTIVATIONAL CONCEPTS

Throughout this book we have seen how individuals use motivation in supervising employees and in managing groups This chapter will focus on some specific applications of particular motivational concepts.

Teaching Machines

One application of a simple motivational model is the *teaching machine.* The teaching machine uses the principles of reward and repetition which are derived from stimulus-response learning. The teaching machine presents relatively small pieces of information and then asks the learner to answer questions about the information. If an answer is wrong, the learner will be referred to more information which explains why the answer was incorrect, and then asked to answer again. If the answer is right, new information is presented. The teaching-machine principle is also used in programmed textbooks, but in book form rather than on a screen. Sometimes, besides the reward of new information for a correct answer, the learner is told "good work" or "right," or (particularly in the case of children) even given a reward, such as a piece of candy. The reward, whatever it is, makes the correct response more likely to occur whenever the appropriate question is asked. Eventually the response is learned and becomes part of the learner's permanent behavior pattern. Teaching machines and programmed textbooks have become important tools in many industrial training situations.

Behavior Modification

Stimulus-response principles are also at work in the newer *behavior modification* systems, in which the learner is rewarded for performing desired behaviors. At first behavior modification was used when individuals wanted to change some behavior pattern they disliked, such as a phobia. For example, instead of enduring rather lengthy psychological treatments for curing a fear of snakes by seeking the initial cause of the fear, individuals simply substituted less fearful, more useful behaviors. Systems were devised by which people could be trained, through rewards, to exhibit less and less panic around snakes. Behavior modification methods were gradually expanded in order to shape other kinds of behavior and more recently have been used in business situations as well. Some examples are systems for rewarding perfect attendance or superior on-time records.

Management by Objectives

Motivational models such as those developed by Herzberg and McClelland are the basis for the concept of *management by objectives*. The basis of the *MBO* idea, as it is called, is that individuals in an organization should know the items on which their performance will be evaluated. Employees, working with their supervisors in a collaborative process, set goals for themselves and time limits for fulfilling them. In this way, people know their goals, feel that they are achievable, and know that their achievements will be recognized. By participating in the setting of objectives, employees learn more about overall company objectives and what their role in them is. More information about MBO will be found in *The Planning Process*, by Brickner and Cope.

Job Enrichment and Job Enlargement

The higher level needs, such as the esteem needs, are the basis for the kinds of programs known as *job enrichment*. The job enrichment idea is an attempt to overcome the motivational problems caused by mass production and mechanization. The partitioning of a production process into small repetitive parts is often efficient in getting work done. However, the resulting routinization of jobs leads to fatigue, boredom, and lack of attention in employees, which in turn may result in high employee turnover, careless accidents, and low productivity. Thus routinization may not always achieve the high rate of production intended.

A forerunner of job enrichment is *job enlargement*, which simply involves giving a worker more pieces of the job to do, or permitting the employee to exchange jobs with another person. Job enlargement was tried after research studies found that workers who did more than one job (such as maintenance people, or "relief" workers who filled in for many people during a day) were less bored and more productive than those whose jobs were repetitive. Job enlargement plans often involve permitting workers to select their tasks for a given time period from the various jobs that must be done. Or workers may be allowed to change tasks every day or even more frequently. While such systems seem to reduce boredom somewhat, their effect on quality or quantity of production is not nearly as strong as that of job enrichment systems.

The real importance of job enrichment goes beyond simple variety. Job enrichment plans assume that workers need to have responsibility and pride in their work. Thus job enrichment must also involve workers' ability to make decisions about their work and to identify with the final product. In job enrichment settings, employees usually work in groups and can assign various tasks among themselves. Sometimes members of one group assemble the entire product, and they can see the results. If this is not possible, they assemble a component considered to be a completed unit, or in some other way can finish a big enough "piece" of work so that they can feel a sense of completion. Experiments of this sort in the Swedish auto industry are well known and have had productive results. In some cases, overall output has increased. More frequently, quality increases have been achieved, as well as significant reductions in absenteeism and turnover (which reduces the cost of training new employees). Job enrichment plans attempt to increase on-the-job fulfillment of needs by providing workers with variety, valuable social relationships, and information about the importance of their jobs and their skills in completing them.

Compensation Plans

McClelland's need-for-achievement concept can be seen clearly in several *compensation plans*. If a company rewards the manager of its most profitable unit with a bonus, the bonus does many things. It provides the individual with more money, of course, to use as an instrument in fulfilling other needs. However, the bonus also represents or symbolizes achievement and lets the manager know that the company values his or her work.

A related program is called *profit sharing*. In a profit sharing plan the company indicates in advance a set percentage of its profits to be put aside for division among employees. Sometimes this "pot" is divided according to each person's base salary; in other situations it is divided according to the profitability of the unit managed by each person. In any case employees have reason to be more concerned with the profitability of their units and of the organization as a whole. If the firm is not profitable overall there won't be any profits to share!

An even more powerful use of motivation is present in plans which involve sharing company ownership. In some cases firms may compensate their employees with shares of stock, or they may sell shares to employees on favorable terms. The employee-owner then has a "stake" not only in his or her own job, but also in the overall success of the company. The individual will then be more interested in the company's reputation, the quality of the product, managerial performance, and the like. Originally ownership plans were limited to management level employees. Now they are frequently applied at all levels in the company. Such a plan strives to make the employees' goals the same as those of the company, by making those goals more important to each individual.

Another motivationally based compensation plan provides rewards for money-saving innovations. The idea is not new—for many years companies have tried to solicit employee ideas through variations on the "suggestion box" system. However, often this method did not work well. Employees assumed (sometimes correctly!) that these systems were manipulative—that employers were not genuinely interested in their ideas. They often felt that only small and unimportant suggestions would be adopted, that good suggestions might be "stolen" (used without credit), or that only token compensation would be given. Now systems based on human resources approaches are being used. These systems recognize

that employee ideas may have real worth, so they are actively
sought. Ideas accepted may involve major changes or investments. Employees who make suggestions are compensated
with a percentage of the actual money saved, so they have
a stake in seeing the change work. Many companies have
introduced such plans successfully. They will succeed if they
are managed so that employees do not feel manipulated.

New Kinds of Employees

Predictions for the future of American business indicate
that the "typical" employee will be a more highly educated
professional or technical specialist. As a result, some organizations are focusing on another kind of individual motivation,
which might be called *career planning*. It involves working
with individuals on a counseling basis to help them determine
and plan for their career goals. Employees can plan their
paths of advancement through the organization, and see what
additional training or experience they may need at various
intervals. Career planning allows employees to set realistic
goals and at the same time enables organizations to improve
their own human resource planning.

Organizational efforts with employee groups outside
the traditional worker "mainstream" use motivational concepts as well. Programs may attempt to move such people
as the hard-core unemployed up the need hierarchy; they do
not focus only on immediate physical needs, in order to encourage regular work habits and a sense of responsibility.
Programs for women, blacks, and other minority groups may
concentrate on teaching behaviors expected by the business
world. Programs for rehabilitated criminals or addicts may attempt to reward new behavior patterns in order to deempha-
size rewards available in a criminal environment. In each case,
the success of a program depends on the ability of its de-
signers to understand the motivation not only of the new
group of workers, but of those already in the work situation.

SUMMARY

We use motivation every day, whenever we make decisions about how to supervise people. However, motivational concepts may also be used more formally in designing programs to make workers and thus an organization more productive. Usually these plans try to reinforce good performance by rewards and to increase employee participation and responsibility. Examples of such programs are teaching machines, management by objectives, job enrichment, and various compensation plans such as profit sharing, bonuses, stock ownership plans, and productivity-suggestion systems.

SKILL DEVELOPERS

1. Talk to someone who has participated in a program using motivational ideas such as the ones described in this chapter. What were some of the problems in implementing such a program and what were some of the results?
2. Imagine that you had the authority and resources to implement one of these plans in your own organization. Which would you select and why?

REFERENCES

PAUL, WILLIAM J., JR.; ROBERTSON, KEITH B.; AND HERZBERG, FREDERICK. "Job Enrichment Pays Off." *Harvard Business Review*, March–April 1969, pp. 61–78.

PANEL DISCUSSION

Here the panelists talk about how they use motivational principles in specific managerial situations.

Bob: Look at Japan; they will give almost their full life to the company, vacation . . .

Jerry: But the theory in Japan is from the cradle to the grave. You go to work for Sony. Your status is you live in Sony village and if you die, the wife is taken care of, but that's a different fraternal thing.

Phil: I guess what I'm saying is that it's great to do all those things.

Bob: But how do you get the thank you's for it?

Phil: I think we ought to focus on keeping the work itself challenging and stimulating and interesting so that they will want to come to work.

Jerry: Let's face it. How in the hell do you keep certain things stimulating? If you're going to put pies in a bag or you're going to put gum drops in a box it's a boring job. Only certain jobs can't be changed.

Phil: Yeah. We're getting into an area of job enrichment almost, right?

Jerry: That's what you're talking about. You've got to be practical about it. There's a lot of things you can do up to a point, but there's some menial jobs; the guy who's going to peel potatoes. He's still going to have to feed the potatoes into the peeler. That's your technology. So instead of peeling with a knife you dump it into a machine and it peels it, but you've still got to load it.

Bob: It's no good to call him a machine operator. That doesn't turn him on at all.

Jerry: So we don't call them janitors. We call them sanitors.

Phil: I think one of the things, if you want to talk about young people in terms of their orientation toward the work now, is they're also looking at the job itself. "What constitutes the job here? Are there any areas where I can be successful, where I can experience achievement?" I think that should be one of our changes in business or in industry. They try to make the jobs, whenever possible, worthwhile. I agree with you and I agree with Bob. There are some jobs that are virtually unenrichable.

Jerry: But you try; you know what I mean.

Phil: But you try. You can do some things in an imaginative combination.

Phil: Change the work hours, you can vary some of the hygiene factors a little bit.

Bill: You can move people around.

Lynne: Excuse me. We're talking about the kids today, saying, "Give me more, give me more, you owe me something." Maybe that's what we're doing with the benefits. We're trying to fulfill that need for the freebies.

Phil: I think the benefits too often substitute for worthwhile jobs. That's not necessarily bad. It used to be if you wanted to keep people happy on the job you'd find a new gimmick. More time off and some more money. I wonder now if people always buy that. I think the work itself should be reasonably worthwhile and it sounds corny and head-trippy but it should be meaningful. But on the other hand, you've got companies where some of that work should be automated. But you can't afford to. So you've got to hire people to do it.

Jerry: Then you create all sorts of problems. If you start automating everything, I mean this is what's happening. You've got all the work force coming into play. That's why you don't have any problems in China. They do things primitively and archaically, but everybody's got a job and they don't have welfare.

Phil: But I guess the question is, can we slow down technology? Can you integrate technology with human needs?

Jerry: If you knock off the menial job what are you going to do with these people? So you can't knock off these menial jobs. I think the name of the game is "Planning." You've got a hell of a problem, though.

Bill: The first line supervisors who are going to be reading this book have got this problem of supervising what we would call meaningless jobs. Many of the jobs would appear to be relatively routine and repetitive and yet we are faced with, "What does he do to motivate his people?" I'll carry that one step further—what would be the possibility of him coming in and saying to his plant superintendent, "I want to move all my people around. Now it may not be the most efficient way because they're going to have to go through a new learning process, but I feel there's going to be a pay off down stream," or "I'll de-automate something, take out some of the automation in order to make a job more meaningful."

Jerry: Well, if meaningful also helps the bottom line in the efficiency, then it's worthwhile. I know for a fact we did exactly that in our operation. We just rotated the girls in the wrapping lines so every hour or every two hours one girl was indexing pies while two girls were packing them. They just worked around the clock and they kept switching. Just by switching boxing pies from the left side to boxing pies on the right, just that simple switch breaks the monotony. You go through the regular bit of piping in music, then you take off Muzak, then put an FM station on and then you change to different stations. So basically you're breaking up the monotony as much as you can. It's a diversionary thing. The job is basically monotonous, so you try to make it look like it's not monotonous by just changing physical positions.

Phil: I think that there are probably some partial solutions that a manager or supervisor might take to make the job at least bearable. One is to use them as entry level jobs. For example, "Harry, this is the job. It's bagging peanuts. The best thing about the job is that you're going to be on it for six months and after that, assuming you've made our other objectives, you move on." You might use it; for example, you might rotate the jobs as Jerry's doing. You might ask for volunteers for the dull job. Let's face it. Maybe you've had a rough night the night before and bagging peanuts is about all you're up to that day so you bag the peanuts. Another aspect might be to hire the handicapped for some of those jobs. Too often our personnel departments screen out people because they don't meet minimum standards and yet we don't need super-qualified people.

Bill: And they might be very motivated on these jobs, because it's a job they can do, some skill as versus not being allowed to do anything in our society.

Jerry: And then you get the minorities. You get the ones that have a language barrier. They're thrilled to get the job. First of all, they don't have—you don't hit any inferiority complex because if they don't talk they don't feel inferior. They have a job. It pays well and they're very satisfied with that. Also, you get people who are mentally retarded. They like that simple job, and they have no desire to go on. And some people just like those jobs. I've got a girl who's been with me since 1956. She's been bagging pies ever since and she loves it. I begged her, especially with the EOC coming in, "Please take a foreman's job. Please take a fork lifter's job. Please take a dough mixer's job." She says, "Jerry, I don't want it. I love it. I'm happy."

Phil: That's true.

Jerry: What these young managers should do, if they have a monotonous job on the line, is see if they've got somebody who will be happy with it. There are people who are happy with it. There are people who are happy cleaning houses or cleaning toilets. They don't look at it as a degrading job.

Phil: That's where you can really stress some of the hygiene factors. Then you can play with the Muzak and you can work with the lighting and you can give free lunches.

Jerry: But if you've got a guy who wants to be president he ain't going to be happy bagging pies or peeling potatoes. Not for long.

Sue: But on the other hand, I think there is something related back to social responsibilities. You had talked earlier about getting people committed to the goals of the company, and I think that one way to get them committed is to persuade people you have some decent goals. Perhaps fewer people are committed these days to turning out the most widgets. They don't see that as a company goal they can really identify with. But some social responsibility goals are things people can identify with; and it would seem to me, equally, that even on monotonous jobs there can be pride. We talked about this earlier. Pride in work, particularly if you have pride in what the company's doing. It's maybe easier to peel potatoes if you think a person's going to starve without them than if it's potato chips that are just going to make them fat. I don't know. But I think that when people have some understanding of *why* they're peeling a potato, or *why* they're stapling papers. . .

Bob: How it fits into the whole . . .

Sue: I think this is particularly true of office and clerical kinds of things. One place I worked, we had eight floors of clericals who were primarily women at that time. It was a company that made forest products. We had a tour to a logging camp. It was just astonishing. Those women said, "I never knew how what I was doing with all those invoices had anything to do with trees." Well, this wasn't just a hygiene thing. It wasn't just a manipulation of, "Here, let's take you on a field trip"; but it was being able to see the product that all that paper work represented. I don't know whether clerks actually get to see patients or not in your situation . . .

Lynne: We make it a practice of bringing a person into a department and have some orientation there, and then take them out and expose them to what the other departments are doing. Why is that piece of paper that's come back from the laboratory so important? Why do I have to put it on the right chart? If they see the full gamut of what's going on from the time the patient enters the system, and right on through, they usually do a much better job. They get along better with people in the other departments too. They have a better understanding of the system—how and why it works.

Bill: You work in a critical service industry, health and hospital. Do you feel that your people that work for you even though they're in clerical jobs sense that their activities might be perhaps more valuable, more meaningful than in some other type of operation, or is that ever expressed to you?

Lynne: They come into the organization with that in mind, but then they become callous too. Pretty soon it wears off and you try to remind them how very important this work is.

Bill: You think the initial attraction was because you're in the business of saving lives.

Phil: That's, I think, a good practical incentive that a supervisor has, to brief people on the importance of their job and how the interrelationship of their job can save the company objective.

Bob: And particularly if you've got a natural like Lynne has. The health service and the critical industries—that you ought to play on that for motivation.

Lynne: I really think that something that we have to bear in mind is that we're not totally responsible for the other human beings. That each employee has the responsibility for himself, and I'm not God and I'm not going to make Sam's world or Jane's world perfect for them.

Phil: That's right.

Lynne: I can offer them comfortable working conditions and reasonable benefits. But then that man has responsibilities too.

Bill: I think that's an enormously important point. In this kind of conversation you can get lost in the other side of the coin. But everybody must recognize that they have to take personal responsibility for themselves. That's where the ultimate responsibility drops off. That's where the buck stops. If you're going to be miserable in this world, it's not so much your environment, it's how you've positioned yourself and that's certainly true, I think, in our kind of a society in the United States. Perhaps here more than in anyplace else. If you don't like what you're doing it's probably because you've taken the actions and you've followed the path that has led you to this point. You'd better start thinking about what is it that makes you tick and how can you change your behavior to position yourself some place else?

Lynne: I really can't get too terribly excited about morale, per se. I think that there are other things that make morale go down. Or allow it to stay down. If you offer pleasant working conditions and training and that individual still is not happy he's possibly misplaced or chooses to be unhappy.

Bill: I think that's something the young, first line manager has to recognize too—that there are these terrific extremes and you can put in 90 percent of your time in just a relatively limited number of people and you're going to get a very small amount of results, whereas spreading two-thirds of that time over the rest of the people will increase your output because of your ability to motivate them enormously.

Lynne: I think a lot of people go into management with the idea in their minds of playing God and the power that they can have over other people's lives, and then in turn feel guilty when they don't make it with the other people, and when other people don't make it. I think you have to look at yourself and how you're approaching life. Do you really want to control other people?

Bill: There's a test that they give managers, called the FIRO-B test that illustrates what your control needs are and how you express that. You see a lot of managers have a very high score on wanting to control other people and conversely very, very low scores on wanting to be controlled. That's again all a part of this question of getting insight into yourself.

Phil: That's right.

Sue: I find this is, in teaching, one of the things you notice most—that people have the hardest time aligning how they want to be managed with how they want to manage. And it's an incredible "us" and "them" situation, and "them" is always one line below me. *I* want to participate. *I* want to be involved. *I* want my opinion to be asked but "they" don't. I want to control them, in other words; but I don't want to be controlled.

eight

A Final Note

The question "How can I motivate employees?" does not really have a simple answer. We have seen that in one sense, the answer is, "You cannot. Employees already have needs and goals inside them; you can only work with them." Another answer is, "You can create a climate in which employees are motivated toward organizational goals through the use of influence and rewards." There are many other variations on this response as well.

Still, the ability to understand and use motivational principles is a most important managerial skill. With this ability, you can diagnose many organizational problems. You can develop alternative solutions and weigh them in light of what you know. Perhaps most importantly, you can make a decision or institute a change with the ability to foresee the consequences of your actions. All this requires only the knowledge you have gained, plus your own understanding of the particular setting in which you work. Since no two settings are exactly alike, there are no easy "how to do it" rules which can be automatically applied. But all managerial problem solving involves the necessity to take available knowledge and information and interpret it with regard to a specific problem.

Occasionally we have hinted at another question, "Where do we go from here?" It seems possible that changes in society will change the characteristics of people who work. Will this alter our ability to apply motivational knowledge? We know that people will always have motivation. It is likely, however, that if the workforce of the future is better and more technically educated, we will see more higher-level needs expressed, on the job, with a reduction in expression of needs such as safety and affiliation, which organizations have traditionally tried to satisfy. Therefore, application of specific motivational programs may have to change drastically. Concepts of social responsibility and ethics in business, including concern for the physical or natural environment, also reflect a growing representation of higher-level needs.

We have seen reflected here a final set of questions as well. It is easy to move from "How do I motivate employees" to "How do I motivate my boss?" or "How do I motivate my spouse/child/friend?" or "How can I motivate myself?" These are areas for you, the reader, to explore more fully now that you have motivational information and tools at hand.

In the last few pages, you will hear the panelists considering these questions. Then, at the end, each of them will describe what he or she believes is the hardest motivational problem to solve.

PANEL DISCUSSION

Lynne: I can take care of myself in the world as far as the business end of it is concerned, but certainly I have other needs. I enjoy companionship and have a great need for companionship.

Sue: I was responding more to what Jerry said about being able to be independent. I heard you as saying a much more individualistic thing about people being able to . . .

Jerry: No one is saying that you haven't got a need. I encouraged my wife into getting into business, because I felt it was a good outlet for her; and fortunately I'm a little more mellow than she is because it's a new experience for her. And her job and everything is a big traumatic thing, and I don't pooh-pooh it, you know. I've been through that so many times; but to her it is a big thing; and if I just sluff it off it's going to seem like I have a superior attitude.

Bill: Well, that's the only reality we have—it's what we perceive.

Jerry: O.K., so you have to make her happy, but eventually, down the road in a couple of years, she'll look back and say, "God, what a ridiculous thing. I was all uptight about that." But right now it's a big thing.

Lynne: But it's the same with employees. Their problems are just tremendous to them.

Jerry: That's right. Everything is big and traumatic and catastrophic, and you've got to calm them down; and that's basically what a manager is.

Lynne: Well, I think we accept where they are, "Yes, that is a big problem to you," but not fall apart at the seams yourself over it, even if you are feeling like falling apart.

Jerry: Well that's what managers do—good managers. I guess that's what I meant by "Big Daddy," because you've been through there and you've been through the chairs so you're more or less holding their hand. You listen, and then you calm them down, and then you get them to look at it in the proper perspective, which they can't do at the moment.

Lynne: I don't know that I necessarily agree with you that you get them to look at the proper perspective. You help guide them.

Bob: You try to put it in perspective, what's proper from where you're at and I'm at.

Phil: But the way that you get them out of that funk is to have them focus on the organization's goals, and it's hard if they're more preoccupied with their own problems. That's a very delicate tightrope to walk. You know if you spend all your time social-working employees you're never going to get this job done.

Bob: I've got happy employees, but the bank won't loan me any money.

Sue: I had a friend once who was an office manager for an organization that ran T-groups, and she said it was very frustrating because you couldn't just say to one of the clerks, "Here, file this letter." You would say, "I have a very meaningful job for you, and it's very important to the organization that you do this, and thank you for your participation."

Phil: "Now don't you feel good after you file that?"

Sue: Yeah, everybody was so attuned with this way of dealing with other people. She had come up through the T-group ranks; she was not a professional manager. She said she began to understand what the contrast was between making people happy and getting the job done. I think this is back to that manipulation question we brought up a little earlier—that people can detect when something is being done simply to make them happy and people don't always expect to be happy if they're used as resources. They're going to be satisfied for the most part even if they're not delighted all the time.

Bob: That's one of the things I do perceive in the younger people—that they almost do feel that life owes them a certain level or stance of happiness. You know, they are happy. It is somebody else that's wrong. Not themselves, but the corporation or the government or whatever. I do see that.

Lynne: But how did that happen to them, then?

Bob: Our society.

Lynne: I see this in my own children. They get a fantastic job and then decide you want to go fishing. "Oh, well, that's alright, he'll understand."

Bob: "I *want* to go fishing."

Phil: Come to think of it, I can relate to that because I think my folks owe me a hell of a lot!

Sue: This is the final legacy of the depression; the people spent so much time with unfulfilled needs they vowed their children would not have unfulfilled needs, and therefore created in them the expectation that their needs would be fulfilled.

Bob: We've fulfilled their physical needs. We've given them cars, money, and things like that; and yet we hear our kids by their behavior say, "There were some love needs and some emotional needs that we weren't getting while you were out striving for all those things—you kinda deprived me of certain things."

Lynne: They had the expectation that those needs should be filled.

Bill: Is that now the role of managers? Since we have a work-force that is increasingly being composed of younger people, is one of the methods of motivating people going to be to try to meet some of these unfulfilled needs on the job?

Jerry: Well, I'll tell you one thing. If you're going to get managers you're going to find if you're interviewing people, they're going to ask you what the living conditions are and what's the schooling.

Bob: How often will I be relocated? How often am I going to be jerked away?

Jerry: And if they have a choice, sometimes they will take a lower-paying job, working in a better environment, and because they are involved with ecology and the environment. I'll be honest with you—when I went into the business world, I wasn't that concerned; but I became aware because of the publicity and what was happening. I think it's very good. I think we've got a crop of young, good people; but thank God we got through this acid age, and I think we're getting to live with the nuclear situation. It's permeating their heads that there's not going to be a nuclear war, or the chances of one are not going so great so that fear of nuclear war is no longer there as it was 5 or 10 years ago. That's helped the environment. Outside forces had a tremendous influence on the environment, especially on management.

Bob: Almost every young family that you do hire today is a two wage earner family and that means there's a lot more interrelationship—you can't deal with just the husband. And also they see themselves therefore as having more alterna-tives.

Jerry: So you have to deal with them; no, the club isn't the bucks any more. Because they don't need it. Because if I'm out of work the old lady's working and nobody's knock-ing down the door for paying the rent so we're in good shape. So, they're dealing from a little different level. It's a challenge for us and we've got to be realistic. The problem is, in these large corporations, the old guys. I mean guys in their 60's, on the way out, who remember the old days when everybody was putting 18 hours in, and when the President came by they snapped to attention and if you worked for "Old Glory" that was good enough, and don't worry "Old Glory" will take care of you. The young kids say, "I don't care if you're on the Fortune 500. What is in it for me and what are you doing?" Which is healthy, but hard for the chairman of the board, who's 60, "What do you mean, he's asking for a raise? What do you mean he wants this?" They're going to have to understand but they don't like it. I've had some heavy run-ins, but I said, "Do you think Del Monte's the only company around? There's other companies that are just as secure for these young people; why in the hell should they come to Del Monte or General Motors?" This is a new ball game and I think it's good. But it's pretty hard to change a guy who's been there for 35 years.

. . .

Jerry: I'd like to bring out something that I've had in the back of my mind. One of the things that made me run and I'd like to get some discussion on it. In my early stages, one of the things that motivated me to be "successful" quote, if I'm successful, is that I was always afraid of failure. In fact, I've had some discussions on this and people thought I was nuts, but I always felt that the only reason I was successful was because I feared failure, and if I failed it was because of my own inability and I wouldn't accept that and I always pushed. Psychologically, I just couldn't accept failure and I couldn't tolerate it.

Lynne: You're not perfect; how do you cope with those occasions when you're not at your very best?

Jerry: No, I think it has nothing to do with very best. It's just that I wouldn't accept failure.

Lynne: But you can't always win.

Bob: That doesn't mean every little idea.

Jerry: No, I mean overall. I opened up a big plant in Los Angeles. I was in the hole after 9 months; my total net worth was 500 bucks. And I owed $70,000 and at that time it looked like nine hundred billion dollars. How was I going to pay these poor people back? 'Cause it's my word; I owed them this money, and I just said, "What did I do wrong?" and I just kept on working; I just can't fail and you have that goal, like they talk about the runner. When he gets down to that home stretch he's got that extra sprint.

Phil: The adrenalin.

Lynne: Are you saying that you accepted at one point that you hadn't made the right decision or that you'd gotten into a bad situation?

Jerry: No, but there was something I was doing wrong. "Why isn't this thing going?"

Lynne: But you did look at it and decided that you had made a mistake.

Jerry: No, I became doubtful. That's when it was critical for me and that's when all of a sudden that inner feeling came on. You just can't throw the sponge in, 'cause then you're a quitter.

Sue: You know, Jerry, there is some interesting research that's been going on. It actually got started with a question about women and motivation. They had all this problem trying to make the need for achievement data fit women. You could find all these men who had high need for achievement, but when they gave the same tests to women they got weird answers. It turned out that they were finding a whole new classification of the answers in which people did things because they were afraid to fail or interestingly enough, also, afraid to succeed. Many women in our society, rather than being taught that success has positive consequences, were taught that it has negative consequences. If you're first in your class none of the boys will date you. But this whole idea of fear of success and fear of failure as related motivational concepts is now beginning to emerge and what makes Sammy run may be in fact the fear of the tiger that's going to devour him if he fails.

Bob: You run away from something as hard as you run towards it.

Sue: I did some research on this myself where people had to answer by writing a description, and it's amazing how strongly those answers stand out. For a person who doesn't have that feeling it's hard to imagine, but you read one of these answers and the person is saying, "If I don't make it, here are all the dreadful things that will happen to me." It's a phenomenon that's apparently been there, but hadn't been studied.

Jerry: Under the surface.

· · ·

Sue: I'd like to hear any comments as to whether the things you've said about what you're doing in a managerial role are the same types of motivations that you would use in your homes with your husband, boyfriend, wife or whoever.

Bob: Unfortunately not enough.

Jerry: You're dealing with human beings, and you have goals also at home. You have goals for your wife and you have goals that you set for your children and for yourself, essentially the same ball game, just using a different thrust or a different, you know. So instead of getting compensation, you get pleasure. I think that's your payoff.

Bill: But we miss that sometimes, though. That's the reason I made that point. We're operating as managers or supervisors in two different worlds and we have to put on a different hat when we go into one or the other, and my own feelings are that's dysfunctional—that you have to see yourself as different.

Bob: Particularly around the area of communication.

Jerry: But the biggest problem, you know, you're talking about personal life, is when you have a fairly strong personality and then you come home and the wife says . . .

Bob: "Take out the garbage."

Phil: You say, "Wait a minute; I'm an executive."

Sue: "I'm going to supervise somebody else taking it out."

Jerry: You have a cocktail party to go to and you have a business meeting scheduled and she says, "Cancel the business meeting," and then the realization, "Well, I'm number two in your business."

Bob: "Have to be in early tonight. I've got a big meeting in the morning."

Jerry: So that's pretty heavy, and that's where the family conflict comes in. This is something that you've got to get straight and it's not easy.

Phil: One of the other areas where there is some applicability between what we're talking about here, especially in the realm of communications, is the constructive expression of anger. For example, when you talk with your wife or your husband or your boyfriend and you get angry, it should be a specific incident that you can relate it to. We talked about it here as far as disciplinary counts.

Lynne: I was just thinking about my own experience with my children. About six months ago I was totally bored with what I was doing. I knew that I was capable of doing more; and consequently I was meddling so much in their lives that they couldn't breathe, and I was a Jewish mother on top of them all the time. Nagging them half to death, and now I am more fulfilled in what I'm doing and I kind of leave them alone and they're not doing so badly on their own.

Bob: They come home and say, "Mom, it's nice to have you happy."

Jerry: I've had my kids come up to me and say, "We want to talk to you." I say, "Look, I don't think we should talk tonight. I've had a very rough day, and it's really nothing against you, but I don't think I could be objective and I'm not really in a good mood. Now can it hold? But if it's imperative I'll talk to you." And this is the way we've got it with our kids, because the kids run into your bedroom, and they start rattling off and they don't ask how *you* feel. They take it for granted. Dad's home and we can discuss this with him. They've been waiting there since 3:00 o'clock and you walk in at seven. They pounce on you.

Lynne: That's important to them.

Jerry: I realize that. That's why you've got to get it right. You say, "Look, is it important? I'm not up to it, but if it's that important we'll deal with it."

Bob: I'd take a look at their faces and say tell me something good. They halt on their heels. Daddy needs to hear something good.

Sue: I think relating to personal life, I find it's a lot easier to practice what I preach at work where I can get away from it than at home. I'm tempted to be much more manipulative with my family and my friends than I am with colleagues, and I find that kind of scary because one would like to think that one's more collaborative with the family where you have a more trusting and more permanent relationship. Sometimes it doesn't seem to work that way.

Bob: Speaking about personal life, it's also 3:00 o'clock.

Sue: I would like to ask you one more thing and if every body doesn't want to answer or if you can't think of anything, O.K. What is the most difficult situation in which to motivate people or what is the most difficult kind of person to deal with motivationally?

Bob: Bad times and unhappy people.

Jerry: Or, here's a heavy one. Here's a person who's got tremendous ability. He can go beyond his present job but has no desire.

Bob: You can't find the button. He may have desire, but not that you can find.

Jerry: No, no. I disagree with you. I have a specific person. All he wants to do and he's always threatening to do, is get himself a little damn service station and little donut shop and $300.00 or $400.00 a month someplace in Oregon by the seashore so he can go fishing. But he's too hungry for the buck to give up the job and he's got tremendous ability.

Bob: Put him on a five-year program where he can make enough to buy that little place up there.

Jerry: No, he won't do it even then. Because he won't give up the bucks. He's too young a guy. So how do you motivate people who don't want to be motivated?

Lynne: I find it hardest to motivate people that don't think like I do.

Jerry: Oh, well, you've got to broaden your base.

Lynne: Their style or ideas appeal to me and vice versa—then we have a good thing going. But if they're coming from an entirely different environment, if their goals are different than I think they should be, then I have a problem.

Jerry: Yeah, you do have a problem.

Lynne: I think that there's a lot more that comes in, this is what I expect, this is my style.

Phil: The toughest person to motivate is the person who reached the top of the job in terms of pay and responsibilities and is really peaked out in terms of his usefulness. How do you keep that person involved and motivated?

Bob: I think in bad times on a losing team. That is when motivation becomes the most difficult and there are certain people in life that the sun is always too hot, and the floor is always too hard and they're always just negative, negative, negative. That is like cancer. It grows, it spreads and that kind of person is very difficult to motivate at all, and generally fear is the only way you can motivate him. "Shut up, do your job, don't talk to people or I'm firing your ass."

Lynne: O.K., we'll back up. You were talking about the goals you were putting on your family. And I'm relating to that comment too, because I have expectations of people. I know what I think the goals are. But if that individual's not in tune with me and where I'm going, or where I think we should go, then that presents a problem.

Jerry: That's right. But so be it. You just have to accept and then acquiesce.

Sue: I don't think it's fair to say, "You shouldn't have that problem." The fact is that that is a problem that a lot of us face. That's why a lot of people don't get along with their children.

Phil: 'Cause I have difficulty with people who don't agree with me, whose life style is completely alien and foreign to mine, and I think you have to try harder. You've got to just work with them and you find after a while that you begin to understand where they're coming from.

Bob: Yeah. Maybe a composer, maybe a certain book, and you'll find some thread. Go from there.

Lynne: It takes more of an effort.

Bill: Because they know when you're coming around.

Bob: Yeah. Because they know when you're trying, 'cause they feel the same way.

Lynne: They're receiving some acceptance and vice versa.